Colonial Michilimackinac

STATE · HISTORIC · PARKS

Mackinac State Historic Parks
Mackinac Island, Michigan
© 2000 Mackinac State Historic Parks

ISBN 911872-74-4 soft cover
ISBN 911872-75-2 hard cover

First Edition

First Printing   5,000 copies, soft cover
                 2,000 copies, hard cover

Text: David A. Armour

Editing: Karen McCarthy
Art Direction: Thomas Kachadurian

LEFT: Michilimackinac, an eighteenth-century fortified town, was surrounded by a wooden palisade and guarded by soldiers. RIGHT: Smoking was popular and soft stone was carved into decorative pipe bowls.

Contents

Introduction

MICHILIMACKINAC – The place of the "Great Turtle" has attracted people for thousands of years. From the Native hunters who stalked their quarry near the retreating glaciers to today's tourist talking with a costumed interpreter, people from all over the world have come together at Michilimackinac. Some came to harvest the abundant natural resources; others came to trade. Still others came to conquer. Many came simply to enjoy the beautiful surroundings.

These diverse people met up with each other at Michilimackinac. Some discovered that they had common interests, such as trade. Others burned with hostility and anger. Some stayed for only a few hours or days. Others stayed a lifetime.

This book is about the people who gathered together at Michilimackinac. Their coming and interaction left a rich historical legacy punctuated by exciting events. Michilimackinac cast its spell over everyone, creating rich memories and a compelling desire to return.

LEFT: Carved stone animal effigy. BELOW: Odawa warrior. RIGHT: Native peoples fashioned canoes, shelters, and many other items from birch bark.

The First People

PEOPLE FIRST CAME to the Michilimackinac area when the great glacial ice sheet slowly retreated northward. Their numbers were few and they left few traces of their passing: a piece of chipped flint here, a shard of broken pottery there.

As the lake level rose and fell during the past fifteen thousand years, it left ancient beaches whose ridgelines are apparent today. Approximately 2,500 years ago, the landscape assumed the familiar pattern we see today.

Native peoples were attracted to the Straits of Mackinac during the summer to fish for the abundant whitefish and lake trout. Sometimes they stayed long enough to plant a crop of corn. Many passed by in birch bark canoes, bobbing over the waters of the two huge lakes that join together at Michilimackinac. Some carried copper nuggets from Lake Superior deposits; one buried a small cache for safekeeping. When one of their band died, the people chose as the final resting-place for the body the sacred Island of Michilimackinac, or "Great Turtle," named for its shape.

The unusual rock formations in the Mackinac area gave rise to stories repeated by elders around flickering campfires or during long winter nights inside a snug bark lodge. The teller described how the world had been created here by the Great Hare Michibou (whose name is still attached to the great limestone hill Rabbit's

Back). Other tales spoke of the Great Turtle upon whose back the world rested.

The people called themselves "Anishnabeg." They believed that the land was sacred and that they were responsible to protect the physical and spiritual environment.

Uncounted seasons passed. People came and went. Some camped on the islands now called Mackinac, Round, and Bois Blanc. Others erected their lodges on the mainland on both the north and south sides. Their stories were passed down through generations in the oral traditions of the various peoples, woven into their tales of the natural and the supernatural. The names of individuals are unknown, but tribal names have become place names. Chippewa Point, on the south side of the Straits, was named for the word that later Europeans used to describe the local Anishnabeg – Ojibwa or Chippewa. Iroquois Point, on the north side, recalls a people who spoke a completely different language from the Ojibwa. The Iroquois came to Michilimackinac from several hundred miles to the east as a raiding party in search of prisoners, scalps, and plunder. The distant warriors were defeated, but the site of the battle bears their name.

The story of Michilimackinac is interwoven with the stories of the lives, the beliefs, and the struggles of these people, the first to come to this land.

BELOW: Native people traded their furs for brightly colored cloth and clothing. ABOVE RIGHT: The French came in large canoes heavily laden with merchandise to trade. BELOW RIGHT: The Straits area has been a hub of commerce since the first Europeans came.

Strangers from the East

THE RECORDED HISTORY of Michilimackinac began when people with white skin, strange dress, and an incomprehensible language arrived in the 1630s. Native peoples from the East brought them in birch bark canoes. The French had established a small outpost at Montreal, on the St. Lawrence River, and were searching for an all-water route to Asia and for gold, silver, and other riches. Jean Nicollet led a group westward through the Straits of Mackinac in 1634. They journeyed as far as Green Bay, Wisconsin and returned to Montreal through the Straits.

Though he did not discover Asia, Nicollet brought back with him word of the vast country and the abundance of furs he had seen. During the seventeenth century furs were very fashionable in Europe as collars and coats.

Beaver pelts were especially sought-after to make into stylish men's hats. Merchants in Europe were willing to pay a high price for prime furs. Fur was light in weight, did not spoil easily, and had a high value per pound.

Native hunters in the Great Lakes area obtained furs as a by-product of their quest for food. Men trapped the animals and women skinned, stretched, and dried the hides to make into leather or fur blankets. Because fur was plentiful, the Native peoples did not value it highly. They were delighted to give it to the white traders

from the East in exchange for the much more useful iron tools and multi-colored beads.

Some Native peoples journeyed the hundreds of miles to Montreal to obtain more of these goods. Their coming inspired some of the Frenchmen to go into the interior to trade in the Indian villages. The French authorities attempted to keep the trade within Montreal, but a few French traders, without obtaining permission, set off to find the land of bountiful furs.

Pierre-Esprit Radisson and Médard Chouart des Groselliers were two such rogue traders. During the 1650s, they took their canoe men to Mackinac to trade. They were welcomed by the Indians and returned with canoes heavily laden with prime furs. The French authorities were furious and threw them into jail, but they had opened the door to the upper lakes and displayed its riches to Europe. Others secretly loaded

RIGHT: Fish attracted Native people to the Straits and was an important part of the diet for everyone at Michilimackinac. OPPOSITE RIGHT: Archaeological excavations at Michilimackinac have revealed many remnants of the past. This brass crucifix was probably lost by one of the many Catholic inhabitants.

canoes with cloth, mirrors, knives, hatchets, and a few guns and kegs of brandy, and paddled up the Ottawa River to the west. These illegal traders, called *coureurs de bois* or "woods runners," melted into the forest, where they frequently lived for many years or sometimes for the rest of their lives.

Few names of *coureurs de bois* are recorded, because their lives merged with the Native peoples who lived in the upper lakes country. In order to conduct their trade, they needed the friendship and protection of the Native peoples. The few French *coureurs de bois* lived among thousands of Indians speaking many different languages. The Native peoples welcomed the traders in order to gain access to the power of their unusual objects. However, they were also concerned that the strangers were bringing a profane intrusion into the sacredness of the land. In order to make the traders a part of their community, the Natives sometimes formalized the relationship with a ritual of adoption into a Native family. The traders took on some styles of Native clothing and personal adornment. A daughter of the family was often provided to the trader as a companion, to prepare his food and make and repair moccasins. Some of these relationships were brief; others lasted a lifetime.

From these unions emerged the "Métis," or mixed-blood people. Half Native and half French, the Métis were connected to both cultures. Boys tended to identify with their fathers' background by wearing some French clothing and learning to speak French as well as the language of their mothers. Girls patterned their lives after their mothers by wearing Native dress and speaking only the Native language. If the father deserted them, as was often the case, the children stayed with their mother and easily blended into the Native lifestyle. Their lighter skin was no liability in tribal cultures, which frequently added to their numbers by adopting people of different tribes.

Not all Frenchmen were interested in furs. France was a Catholic country and a number of people were very eager to bring their Christian faith to people who had never heard their gospel. Some of the most devout and dedicated joined the Society of Jesus (known as Jesuits), founded by St. Ignatius Loyola. Jesuits were highly educated, disciplined, and eager to share their faith. When the French came to Canada in the early 1600s, a few Jesuits went to live in the long houses of the Huron people. Known as "Black-robes" for their distinctive dress, they lived with the Huron, studied their language and culture, and taught them about the love of their God.

During the 1640s, raiding Iroquois warriors attacked the Huron. Some of the Jesuits were killed and many of the Huron villages and cornfields were destroyed. The surviving Huron refugees fled west in search of safety. A few Jesuits accompanied them, first to the shores of Lake Superior and then in 1670 to the island then called Michilimackinac. Father Jacques Marquette, a thirty-three-year-old Jesuit priest from

ABOVE: Known as "Blackrobes" for their distinctive dress French Jesuit missionaries lived with the Native peoples and studied their language and culture. OPPOSITE: The Native people had a taste for alcohol that traders were willing to satisfy. The bottle and brass tap were excavated at Michilimackinac.

Laon, France, was with them. After one winter on the Island, the Huron moved their long houses to the mainland around the bay on the north side of the Straits. Marquette followed them and established a small mission at St. Ignace to minister to his flock.

There was already a village in this area, inhabited by a few hundred Odawa (or Ottawa). Like the Huron, the Odawa were refugees: they had recently moved from their homeland, on Manitoulin Island to the east, where they had been in conflict with the Iroquois. The tribe was made up of at least four sub-groups, called Kiskakon, Sable, Sinago, and Nassauakueton. Because they had been active traders, taking furs to Montreal, the Odawa were familiar with the French. The Odawa were proud of their distinctive appearance and pierced their noses for decoration. Their language is similar to Ojibwa, but completely different from Huron. However, the cultures of the Odawa and the Huron were similar. Both groups raised corn to supplement their diet of fish and animals. Both lived in bark-covered multi-family long houses 100-130 feet long, twenty-four feet wide and twenty feet high, with a door at each end. Each of the Huron and Odawa villages was enclosed by log palisades nearly thirty feet high.

Alcohol was unknown to Native peoples before the French brought it to them. They soon developed an insatiable desire for alcohol and would take as much as the French could supply. Traders sometimes increased the quantity of the liquid by diluting it with water and occasionally adding some pepper. With no cultural restrictions, the Natives drank whatever alcohol was available as quickly as possible. Drunkenness resulted and chaos reigned in the village until all the liquor was consumed. During the revelry, people injured themselves and others and some died from alcohol poisoning. Although some traders were frightened, the profits made the experience worthwhile. French traders also liked their alcohol: *voyageurs* always carried a supply of brandy in their canoes for themselves. Many of them eagerly took part in the drunken celebration when they completed their journey to Mackinac.

The French Jesuit priests saw the matter differently. They and the traders had come to Michilimackinac for very different reasons, and though they spoke the same language, they were frequently in conflict. They were sharply divided on the subject of the sale of alcohol to the Native peoples. The priests, appalled by the results of drunkenness among both Natives and traders, tried to get the French government to prohibit the sale of alcohol to the Indians. Many Odawa and Huron leaders also urged the Governor to prohibit alcohol sales to their people. However, when prohibition was periodically enacted, traders always found ways around it. Alcohol remained a problem in the Native communities.

Michilimackinac served as the center for French activity in the upper Great Lakes, and was the jumping-off place for exploration farther west. Late in 1672, Louis Jolliet arrived to lead a government-sanctioned exploring expedition. He recruited Father Marquette, who had established the mission at St. Ignace, to accompany them. In May 1673, Jolliet and Marquette set out in two canoes to find a route to the Mississippi River. Before a month passed, they were paddling that mighty river. They followed it southward far enough to realize that it flowed into the Gulf of Mexico.

The French were not the only Europeans attempting to acquire rich furs in the Great Lakes region. Far to the east of Michilimackinac, English fur traders in Albany, New York offered good prices for prime furs. The colony of New York tried to regulate the trade with Native peoples by confining it to the city limits of Albany, 150 miles up the Hudson River from New York City.

The good prices and quality blankets available at Albany attracted some of the Odawa from Michilimackinac. The Natives told the merchants of Albany about the vast amounts of furs available at Michilimackinac. Eager to make a quick fortune, a group of English traders, headed by twenty-five-year-old Johannes Rooseboom, set out for Michilimackinac in 1686. Paddling eleven canoes up the Mohawk River and down Wood Creek to Oswego, they followed the coastline of Lakes Ontario, Erie, and Huron to Michilimackinac. The Odawa and some of the Huron were happy to welcome them and filled the traders' canoes with bundles of rich furs. Returning safely to Albany, Rooseboom planned a return trip for the following year.

Word of the English expedition spread swiftly among the few French

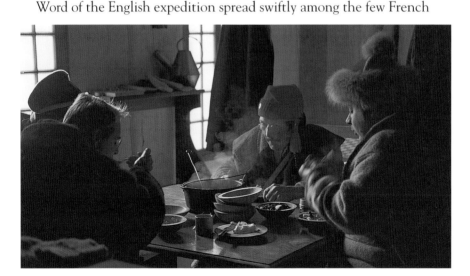

military in the upper Great Lakes. The French claimed exclusive control of the Great Lakes country. When the English returned the next year, they were met by a formidable French force led by Olivier Morel de la Durantaye. The force confiscated the English trade goods and escorted the English traders as prisoners to Montreal. Frightened by the English penetration of the interior, the French authorities blocked the English by constructing a fort at St. Ignace and stationing French soldiers to garrison it. Around 1689, Fort De Buade was built close to the Jesuit mission and the Huron and Odawa villages.

Plans were discussed for blocking the river connecting Lakes Huron and Erie by erecting a fort at Detroit, but it was several years before that was accomplished. In the meantime, French markets began to experience a glut of furs. In 1697, in an effort to reduce the glut, the post of Michilimackinac was closed. French soldiers were withdrawn and the fort abandoned. A new settlement was founded at Detroit in 1701 by Antoine de la Mothe Sieur de Cadillac, former Commandant of Michilimackinac. During the same year, the raiding Iroquois made peace with the French and their Native allies.

Cadillac invited the Native peoples of Michili-

OPPOSITE: Valuable furs at Michilimackinac lured traders far into the interior of North America. ABOVE: French soldiers were sent to Michilimackinac to protect the traders and to keep the British out.

RIGHT: Portable bark shelters allowed the Odawa to move easily from place to place. OPPOSITE TOP: Settling first on the north side of the Straits, the French moved to the southern shore early in the eighteenth century. (*Newberry Library*) OPPOSITE BELOW: The Great Lakes and connecting waterways were a highway for Native peoples and traders.

mackinac to move to the Detroit area. All the Huron and some of the Odawa, led by Outoutagon and LePesant, accepted. Most of the Odawa, under Kinongé's leadership, remained at Michilimackinac, as did the coureurs de bois and the Jesuit priests.

Each summer, when traders and Natives gathered to trade at Michilimackinac, brandy flowed freely. Two Jesuit priests, Fathers Etienne de Carheil and Joseph-Jacques Marest, complained bitterly. They were frustrated by the emigration of their Huron congregation and their limited success in converting the Odawa. The Odawa remained firm in their belief in the powers of the multitudes of Spirits that populated their world. Every time they heard thunder, they stood in awe of the great Thunderbird. When they set out on journeys over the large lakes, they made an offering of tobacco (or sometimes a dog) to Michipou, the underwater panther who lurked beneath the water's surface waiting to devour them. Young people went on vision quests, searching for their special manitou, or protective Spirit. Every warrior carried a bag of objects that connected him to the Spirit world.

Finally, in 1706, the frustrated priests closed the mission, burned the church and residence, and left Michilimackinac to the Odawa and the *coureurs de bois* who came and went. The Odawa also left Mackinac in the winter. The village of 500 souls split up into family groups, which journeyed southward along the western shore of Lake Michigan. The St. Ignace area was deserted. The Native peoples set up winter camps and roamed the woods in search of food and furs. Furs gathered in the winter were thicker and more luxurious, and could be traded for more goods from the French traders. Some traveled as far south as the Grand River and followed it up into the interior. Other families followed the rivers now known as the Muskegon, the Marquette, and the Manistee.

During the summer, the Odawa returned to Michilimackinac to fish and to farm. Since they did not fertilize their fields, the yield decreased in a few years. New fields were created by girdling the trees so they would die. Corn was then planted in the new openings.

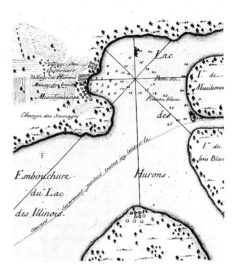

After exhausting the land near the bay at St. Ignace, the Odawa moved their fields west a few miles to Gros Cap. Within a few years those fields also began to wear out. Sometime about 1710, the Odawa, led by Kinongé, old Koutaoiliboe, and Misouaky, relocated their village to the south side of the Straits, near present-day Mackinaw City. There they cleared land for their farms. They built their village without fortifications, since they no longer feared the Iroquois. The fifty-five-year-old French priest, Joseph Marest, who had left the area in frustration,

returned in 1708 and re-established the mission of St. Ignace, to minister to the Odawa. Now he accompanied the Odawa and the *coureurs de bois* across the Straits, bringing the mission with him.

BELOW: Fox warriors resisted French expansion into the western Great Lakes despite repeated military expeditions against them. *(Bibl. Nat. Paris)* OPPOSITE: A modern artist portrays the French settlement built on the south side of the Straits in the early 1700s.

The Straits are Refortified

SEVERAL HUNDRED MILES west of Michilimackinac, in the Wisconsin River valley, there lived a small tribe of Native people who hated the French intruders. Known as the Renards, or the Fox, they had prevented French traders from crossing Wisconsin to reach the vast Mississippi River waterway. Later, the Fox had moved to the Detroit area, encouraged by the French, who wanted to keep an eye on them. But the French, in alliance with the Huron and the Odawa, had attacked the Fox village in 1712 and nearly annihilated it. The survivors fled back to Wisconsin and vowed to fight the French to the death.

The French government in Canada, recognizing the vast wealth of furs in the interior country, decided to rid themselves of this troublesome tribe. Constant Le Marchand de Lignery organized a sizable expedition of soldiers, *coureurs de bois*, cannons, and supplies, and the force rendezvoused at Michilimackinac in 1715. The deserted Fort De Buade was in ruins and the Odawa now lived on the south side of the Straits. Responding to the request of the Odawa and wishing to be close to their trading partners, the French military received permission from the Odawa to erect a small palisade fort on the sandy shore at the present site of Colonial Michilimackinac. The fort contained only a few buildings and was approximately 150 feet long on each side. Soldiers cut heavy logs, then pointed them and set them upright in a ditch to form a defensive palisade wall. Twenty French soldiers garrisoned the fort. The name for the

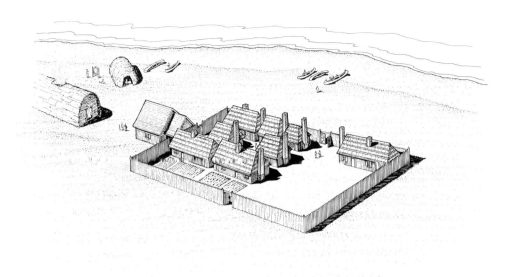

new fort, St. Philippe, was seldom used. Everyone called the place Michili-mackinac. People used the name for the large Island (Mackinac) in the Straits and for the settlement of Indians and Europeans, no matter where the village was located.

The priests from the mission of St. Ignace erected a small chapel just outside the west wall of the palisade so that the Odawa could come to pray without entering the fort itself. Father Joseph Marest stayed at the Straits until 1721, when he was recalled to Montreal. He was sixty-nine years old. His assistant, Michel Guiguas, remained until 1727. After his departure, priests only visited from time to time until the mid-1730s, when Father Pierre Du Jaunay, born in 1704 in Brittany, France, arrived.

The French government built the fort and stationed troops at the Straits in order to maintain military control of the vast upper Great Lakes country, which they called the *Pays d'en Haut* (the Upper Country). They needed a base to supervise the fur trade but also to strike out at the Fox, who refused to enter into an alliance with the French. Expeditions to exterminate them were mobilized in 1715, 1716, 1728, 1730, and 1734, but, despite the considerable expense, the Fox continued to mock the French. Finally a truce of sorts was achieved in 1734.

The Chickasaw who lived near the banks of the Mississippi River also

Beaver was the mainstay of the fur trade. Native people trapped and shot the animals and tore down their lodges to get at them.

troubled the French. Encouraged by English traders from the Carolinas, the Chickasaw resisted the French. In 1736 and 1739 French soldiers and Odawa warriors from Michilimackinac journeyed southward to punish the Chickasaw. Accompanying one of the war parties was a young Métis boy named Charles Langlade. Charles's father was a prominent trader named Augustin Mouet de Langlade who lived at Michilimackinac and kept stables full of animals. Charles's mother, Domitilde, was a sister of the Odawa war chief Nissowaquet, called "La Fourche" by the French. Charles's uncle La Fourche took the boy along with the warriors on the expedition, as was the Odawa custom. Only ten years old, Charles began a career as a fighter that spanned the interior of North America and numbered nearly a hundred battles. Charles eventually married and raised a family at Michilimackinac, and led many military expeditions as a French officer in the *Compagnie Franches de la Marine*. Both he and his uncle played pivotal roles in the history of Michilimackinac.

Langlade's travels were not unique. Both French and Native peoples thought nothing of embarking in open canoes on journeys of hundreds or thousands of miles which took months to complete. Some people lived in nearly constant motion and many passed Michilimackinac numerous times during the course of their lives.

The Odawa Move Away

BY THE LATE 1730s, the agricultural fields of the Odawa near Michili-mackinac were beginning to wear out. It was time to find new lands to grow their corn. The French were distressed by the thought of the Odawa moving far away. They were not only trading partners but also friends and sometimes family. Also, the 180 Odawa warriors, under war chief La Fourche, protected the community from other tribes.

The Odawa elders had their eyes on some good lands along the Grand Traverse Bay. They passed that way each spring and fall, on their way to their winter hunting camps. The French Commandant Pierre-Joseph Céloron de Blainville argued that they should stay near to Michilimackinac. He even offered to send his soldiers to help them clear their fields if they would stay closer to the Straits. The priest Father Pierre Du Jaunay, who had come in 1738 to minister to their souls, also encour-aged them to remain nearby.

Finally in 1742, the Odawa, led by Chief Pen-dalouan, decided to move only about twenty-five or thirty miles southwest to the high bluffs overlooking Lake Michigan. At the top of the bluffs were rolling lands that looked very fertile. Céloron sent his soldiers to help clear the fields and pre-sented the Odawa with a large white French flag to

ABOVE: Maple sugar was an important source of food for both the Odawa and the French. Sap was collected and boiled down in the late winter. OPPOSITE: Ste. Anne's church was the Christian spiritual center of Michilimackinac and its bell could be heard all over the community.

signify their continuing friendship. The Odawa called the area Waganakising or in French *L'Arbre Croche*, The Crooked Tree, because a prominent large crooked pine tree stood atop the bluff and could be seen at a considerable distance by paddlers along the shore. The area is now known as Cross Village. In subsequent years the village moved southward as new fields were needed. Eventually it spread to Middle Village, Good Hart, and Harbor Springs.

Usually the Odawa came and went to Michilimackinac by canoe. However, there was also a narrow trail through the forest connecting the settlements on which the French and Odawa traveled back and forth on horseback. The cordial relationships between the people were occasionally strained when Natives pilfered from gardens and killed a few farm animals.

Father Du Jaunay followed his Odawa congregation and erected a mission church called St. Ignace.

Nearby he cultivated his own farm. The move separated the mission of St. Ignace from the parish church of Ste. Anne at Michilimackinac, so Du Jaunay divided his time between both responsibilities. Because the priest's responsibilities extended beyond these two locations, Father Du Jaunay occasionally went far south to Fort St. Joseph and north to Sault Ste. Marie to perform baptisms and marriages.

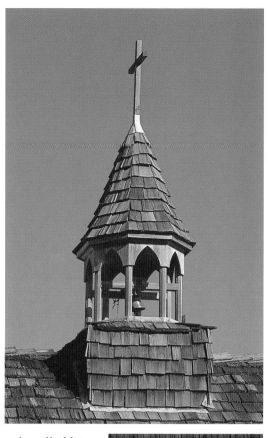

Father Pierre Du Jaunay spent a lot of time talking with the Odawa and learning their language. He painstakingly wrote down their words, compiling a massive French-Odawa dictionary. The Odawa affectionately called him *Le Bec-Jaune*, or "Yellow Beak," and held him in great respect. However, only a few were baptized as Christians. The Odawa were willing to listen to the priest's instruction and respected him as a friend, but the Ojibwa and other tribes, who had no settled villages, paid little attention to the teachings of the Blackrobes.

BELOW: French families provided stability to a small but growing community.
OPPOSITE: The Cross of St. Louis was the most coveted prize for French officers serving in Canada.

Michilimackinac Society

IN THE HUNDRED YEARS since the 1630s, France's holdings in North America had spread from the outpost at Montreal to encompass all of what is now Canada, as well as most of the land along the Mississippi River, called simply "Louisiana." This vast area was called New France.

To supervise the soldiers and the licensed traders in New France, the Governor appointed Commandants to take charge of the forts. The Commandant supplemented his modest salary by trading with the Native peoples. Because a great deal of money could be made trading at Michilimackinac, the position of Commandant there was highly coveted. The post usually was given to a military officer closely connected with the Governor.

Another officer was appointed as second in command. Sometimes the Commandants brought wives and children to Michilimackinac, but frequently they came alone. Occasionally, one of their sons accompanied them so that the young man would gain experience in administration and learn a Native language. Six-year-old Jean-Baptiste-Philippe Testard de Montigny spent two years (1730 to 1732) at Michilimackinac with his father, Jacques Testard de Montigny. Usually, the Commandants maintained large houses in Montreal where their family resided and to which they

returned from time to time. The Commandant was the most important person
at Michilimackinac and he dressed in
expensive clothes to demonstrate his position. Everyone could see in an instant
who he was.

In New France as in France itself, social
classes were sharply differentiated. At the top
were the nobles who came from old families
that were given special privileges by the king.
Believing themselves superior to the people in the
lower classes, they dressed luxuriously (whether or
not they could afford it) to announce their
rank. The king sometimes appointed new
nobles for special services to the government. One of the prizes most sought by military officers in New France was the Cross of
St. Louis, which elevated its holder and his
family into the nobility. Usually, years of dedicated service were required before the award was
presented. For example, Jacques Legardeur de Saint-
Pierre, Commandant at Michilimackinac from 1747 to 1749, did not
receive this award until 1751, when he was fifty years old.

Merchants were beneath the nobles socially but were often wealthier.
They displayed their status by wearing finely made clothes and enjoyed
having people refer to them as *Sieur*, or Sir. The merchants looked down
on the *habitants*, or farmers, who made up the majority of the people in
New France. Although few people at Michilimackinac were farmers, many
of the *voyageurs*, or canoemen, came from farming families.

Permanent settlement meant families. Some men brought their French
wives and families to live at Michilimackinac. The presence of these
women at the Straits solidified French culture by recreating French home
life on the frontier. They taught the French language to both their girls
and boys. Concerned about their families' spiritual welfare, they kept alive
their Catholic religious practices. When Jesuit priests visited the settle-

ment from time to time, the French women welcomed them and brought their children to be baptized.

One of these women was Marie Françoise Alavoine, who, at Montreal in 1709, married Jean Baptiste Chevalier, a thirty-two-year-old trader. They had five children in rapid succession. One died young, before the family moved to Michilimackinac in 1718. During the next seventeen years, eleven more children were born, though, sadly, two of them died. Large families were common in New France, but so was the frequent death of young children.

As the Chevalier children grew to adulthood, the boys generally married Métis or Native girls. The Chevalier women, however, married French men who either lived at or passed through Michilimackinac. Some of the Chevalier children moved back to Montreal but many stayed in the Upper Country. New France was very thinly populated: in 1720 there were only 20,000 French people in the vast area. The whole country resembled a spread-out small town: many people knew each other, and many were related to each other. The extended Chevalier family eventually counted at least 200 members and became prominent in most of the French settlements in the Upper Country, such as Detroit, St. Joseph, and Green Bay.

At the very bottom of the social structure were the slaves, who did not come to Michilimackinac of their own free will. There were a few Black slaves in New France and several came to Michilimackinac, but most slaves were Indians. Referred to as *panis*, some had been captured from the Pawnee tribe, which lived west of the Mississippi River. Most Indian slaves had been captured from other tribes in war. Slavery was common among Native peoples and slaves were usually women and children. A few Native men were enslaved, but it was more difficult to keep them from running away. Women and children slaves helped prepare food and take care of small children. A number of Michilimackinac families owned slaves and some merchants bought and sold a few slaves as part of their business. The

Mackinac parish register book records sixty-nine slaves, both Black and *panis*, including Marianne, Madeleine, Pierre, and Alexander Louis. The whim and kindnesses of the master or mistress determined how miserable a slave's life was. Women slaves were vulnerable to sexual advances from their master or other men. Whether seeking companionship or from force, many female slaves (such as Marie Charlotte in 1746 and Madeleine in 1747) became pregnant and bore children. Sometimes the fathers (such as Charles Chevalier Tellier and Sieur Jasmin, a *voyageur*) were acknowledged, but frequently they were unnamed.

OPPOSITE: **A French ceramic plate found at Michilimackinac** ABOVE: **A brass jaw harp once provided music and entertainment to a Michilimackinac resident.**

The clergy was a small but important class in New France. Their distinctive clothing was recognized by everyone. Though there were several different religious orders in New France, it was the black-robed Jesuits who served as priests at Michilimackinac. All the priests were born and educated in France before coming to North America. A few lay people served as helpers to the priests. Priests occasionally owned slaves, such as the young Black man named Pierre, who belonged to Father Du Jaunay.

At Michilimackinac, Father Du Jaunay had a special business relationship with the blacksmith Jean-Baptiste Amiot, who had come to Michilimackinac shortly after the fort was built. Around 1720, Amiot married a Sauk woman and eventually had eight children. In order to support the work of the church at Michilimackinac, the government had given the priest a monopoly on blacksmithing. The priest employed the blacksmith and took a percentage of his income.

In order to keep watch over the business, the priest located the blacksmith shop beside his own residence. Everyone at Michilimackinac needed the services of the blacksmith. He fashioned a wide variety of objects from iron and brass, including tools for women to use in the kitchen and hinges for the houses. On his anvil he made hatchets and hoes and also sharpened and fixed broken items, including the guns that were so vital to survival on the frontier. The French inhabitants of Michilimackinac were not the only ones who relied on the blacksmith: the Odawa and Ojibwa also needed his services.

The priest employed another craftsman at Michilimackinac, though he did not monopolize his services: master carpenter Joseph Ainse. In 1743, after the community had grown larger, a new church was needed. Joseph Ainse supervised the construction of the solid log-walled Church of Ste. Anne. Named after the patron saint of the voyageurs, the building served as the parish church of the community. Here priests conducted services regularly and celebrated baptisms and weddings. Special feast days – such as that of St. John the Baptist, the patron saint of New France, on June 24, and that of Ste. Anne on June 26 – enlivened the church and the community. Priests recorded baptisms, marriages, and deaths in special register books that still survive in the Church of Ste. Anne on Mackinac Island.

ABOVE: Brass religious medallion with a portrait of Jesus BELOW: Brass thimble is still easily recognizable. OPPOSITE TOP: Michilimackinac ladies prized brass pins. OPPOSITE BOTTOM: Blacksmith at Michilimackinac

Because no Protestants were permitted to emigrate to North America, all French people in New France were at least nominally Catholic. On the frontier, many people ignored religious obligations, but a core of devout parishioners kept the faith alive. Charlotte Ambroisine Bourassa, born in 1735 near Montreal, moved to Michilimackinac in 1743 with her father, René Bourassa, a trader. Charlotte, rather tall with mild brown eyes, was deeply religious and active in church affairs, as was her father. She stood as godmother for the baptism of seven French people, three Natives, six Métis, and eight slaves. On August 12, 1754, when she was nineteen, Charlotte married Charles Langlade, the Métis trader and experienced soldier. Charlotte accompanied Charles when he wintered on the Grand River in the hunting camps of his Odawa relatives. Here their daughter Charlotte was born in 1756.

The Fur Trade

TO PAY FOR THE SOLDIERS stationed at the forts, the government sold trading licenses to merchants. For a sizable fee a merchant was given permission to take a certain number of canoes loaded with trade goods to Michilimackinac or another western post. Montreal, located on the St. Lawrence River which empties into the Atlantic Ocean, was the supply point for all trade to the west. Most of the canoes going to Michilimack-

inac were paddled up the Ottawa River to the Mattawa River, then through Lake Nipissing and down the French River to Lake Huron. The canoes then traveled through the islands dotting the north shore of Lake Huron to Michilimackinac.

Paddling each thirty-five-foot-long birch bark canoe were eight men called *voyageurs* who had signed a contract, or *engagement*, to go to Michilimackinac and return. A bowsman (*avant*) in the front of each canoe watched out for rocks; a steersman (*gouvernail*) in the rear steered the craft. Canoes usually traveled as a brigade with other canoes to provide protection from anyone trying to steal the merchandise and also to help in case of an accident.

Merchandise was packed in bales, boxes, or barrels each weighing approximately ninety pounds. *Voyageurs* carried these containers over the thirty-six *portages*, or "carrying places," between Montreal and Michilimackinac. At each of these *portages*, the muscular young *voyageurs* unloaded the cargo, hoisted it onto their backs, and carried it to the place

where they reloaded the canoe. Sometimes they carried the canoe itself, which weighed several hundred pounds. Other times they dragged the empty canoe with a rope through the rushing rapids. If the rapids were very dangerous or if there were waterfalls, the canoemen would portage around them. They also portaged along paths connecting rivers that flowed in opposite directions. Some "carrying places" were only a few yards in length; others were several miles.

On the big lakes, *voyageurs* kept their canoes close to land so that they could easily reach shore if a sudden squall came upon them. When the weather was windy, they did not venture out. Even with these enforced layovers, the canoes averaged fifty miles per day. Every night the *voyageurs* dragged the canoes up on shore and camped. Meals were simple – usually a thick soup made from dried peas seasoned with a bit of salt pork. Food was the fuel of the fur trade. *Voyageurs* had to carry enough for the long trip to Michilimackinac, because they did not have time to hunt or fish. Dried peas were ideal because they were lightweight and did not spoil. When they reached Michilimackinac and exchanged the trade goods for furs, they refueled for the return journey. Instead of peas, they stocked up on

Traders, who gathered the furs from Native Americans in the wilderness, brought their pelts to the Straits of Mackinac in early summer.

Also in early summer, merchants shipped 90-pound bales of trade goods in large 40-foot-long canoes from eastern cities to the Straits of Mackinac.

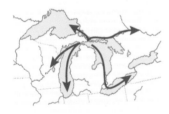

While at the Straits, traders received a fresh supply of goods for another winter of trading, and merchants loaded furs into their canoes for the journey back to the East.

dried corn that had been soaked in lye to remove the hull. The corn was acquired from the local Odawa or, later, from farmers in Detroit. Michilimackinac was a major resupply point both for the canoes returning to Montreal and for the canoes taking the trade goods westward.

At Michilimackinac, thirty-five-foot-long canoes coming from the east met twenty-five-foot-long *Canots du Nord* coming from the north and west. Since it took at least a month to paddle from Montreal to the Straits, merchants usually made only one round trip each season. In exceptional circumstances, there was enough time between the melting of the ice in spring and the refreezing of the rivers and lakes in autumn, and two round trips were possible.

Canoemen from the west were known as *hivernauts*, or "winterers," because they spent winters in Indian villages hundreds of miles to the south, west, or north. They sneeringly referred to those from Montreal as *mangeurs de lard*, or "pork eaters," because they had salt pork in their stew. Western tribes such as Menominee, Winnabego, Sac, Ojibwa, and Sioux also brought furs to Michilimackinac to trade. French traders knew they could get better prices by wintering in the villages but sometimes they could not get government permission to go. The *coureurs de bois* did not worry about permission. They spent their lives with Indian relatives and came to Michilimackinac at will to sell furs and purchase goods for the winter trading.

During the month of July, Michilimackinac was the place to be. Several thousand people came during the summer and sometimes there were more than a thousand all at once. These were loud, boisterous, exciting times – and a bit dangerous. Enlivened by free-flowing brandy and showing off to other canoemen or admiring women, the *voyageurs* laughed, sang, boasted, swore, and occasionally fought.

While the canoemen frolicked, the merchants haggled over the quality of furs or the value of a kettle. Bales of blankets, copper kettles, steel knives, beads, brooches, and ear bobs were repacked into assortments to trade in remote villages. Packs of beaver, otter, muskrat, fox, and other pelts were

The interconnected waterways of lakes and rivers were the highways of the eighteenth century. This 1755 French map shows the Great Lakes country.

sorted, cleaned, and repacked for the Montreal market. Prices rose and fell depending on the prices paid in the Paris auction houses or the shortage of woolen cloth and brandy caused by wartime blockades or shipwrecks. The trade at Michilimackinac was one link in a long chain that stretched from the forests far north of Lake Superior to Michilimackinac, then on to Montreal, down the St. Lawrence River to the Atlantic, across the ocean to France, and then often to the fur markets as far as Germany. Michilimackinac, while remote, was well-known. Beginning in the mid-seventeenth century, its location was indicated prominently on French maps.

Disaster could strike at any moment and a merchant's entire investment could vanish in an instant, but the risk was worth the potential profit. A beaver fur purchased for a few *sols* on the shores of Lake Superior could be sold for many *livres* in Paris and each merchant along the way could make a tidy sum.

Much of the trading took place outside the walls of the fort. Vigilant sentries of the *Compagnie Franches de la Marine* peered over the stockade wall, keeping a lookout for trouble. Indians were admitted into the fort only in small groups and the fort gates were locked up tight each night.

BELOW: Lead seals such as this one from France marked bales of cloth.

Sentries watched for fights between Native peoples. The Ojibwa and Sioux had hatreds that went back generations and the need for vengeance was deeply imbedded in their codes of honor. Because inter-tribal warfare and hostilities would block trade routes, sometimes the Commandant held councils to mediate disputes. During councils it was customary for each group to distribute gifts to the other party to demonstrate

their good will and to emphasize their words. Because Native peoples had no written language they used special belts made from purple and white wampum shells to help remember important decisions. The shells were formed into cylindrical beads about 3/8 inch long, with holes drilled through their length. The beads were joined together with strong cords, forming long strings, or belts that were several inches wide and several feet long. Sometimes figures of people holding hands were woven into the belt to signify peace; a hatchet in the design indicated war.

Councils were lengthy occasions that began with the solemn passing of a sacred pipe carved from red pipestone. Each person in the council took a puff of the pungent tobacco smoke. Native speakers used poetic language, full of symbolism, to convey their meaning. Because tribes such as the Ojibwa and the Sioux did not understand each other and neither understood French, interpreters assisted the conversations and councils. Sometimes several interpreters were needed to translate the message from French to Ojibwa to Sioux and back again. This process took a long time and left open the possibility of grave misunderstandings. The interpreter had a serious responsibility – one word incorrectly interpreted could bring war instead of peace.

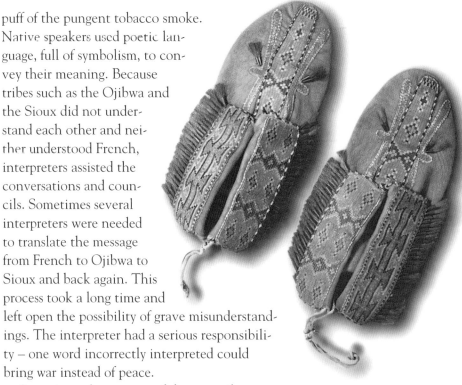

Sometimes the purpose of the councils was to organize for war. The French presence in the interior of North America was contested by some of the Native peoples such as the Fox and the Chickasaw and even the Huron. The French needed allies in these conflicts, so the Commandants at Michilimackinac held councils to mobilize support. On a number of occasions, Michilimackinac served as a rendezvous for military expeditions against the Fox and the Chickasaw. The Odawa had conflicts with these tribes and were eager to cooperate. Sometimes the Ojibwa and the Potawatomi also assisted the French.

The councils were held outside the Michilimackinac stockade while soldiers with loaded muskets watched from the walls. The Native people assembled and sat in a half circle. The Commandant rose and spoke, while an observer recorded his words. A typical speech read: "I was sent to you by your father Ononthio (the Indian name for the Governor of Canada) to tell you he loves all his children, and wishes to give them a token of his love by the presents that I was charged to bring you in his name. But I am also instructed to let him know your views about pledging yourself to raise the hatchet, and to go with your French brothers to fight." After the speech was completed each chief stood and spoke. The Commandant then replied and "had some tobacco given out, and after this distribution had been made, following their custom, they all stood up, formed a circle, and all together gave the war cry; then sat down on the ground crossing their legs in tailor fashion. They painted themselves red and black, and then sang the war song. Some rose and began . . . to march in a circle following each other. . . . After they had danced in this manner the rest of the day and part of the evening, they went to bed. The French remained under arms, and did so during the whole week the Indians stayed with them."

The few French lived among a much more numerous Native population. The French had cannons, and both the Indians and the French had muskets and the skills to use them. The French controlled the supply of gunpowder, but well-placed arrows could still prove deadly. It was the good will of the Odawa, Ojibwa, and other tribes, rather than superior power, that made possible the French presence at Michilimackinac. That good will was fragile and had to be carefully nourished and protected. The French understood this and respected the culture and customs of their Native neighbors, but other people were to come who were not so careful.

OPPOSITE: **Moccasins decorated with dyed porcupine quills** (*Merseyside County Museum*) BELOW: **Brass side plate from a French trade musket excavated at Michilimackinac**

Life at Michilimackinac

BY THE 1740s, the palisades surrounding Michilimackinac had been enlarged several times. As the area prospered, soldiers expanded the original fort to enclose a second row of houses on the land side of the village. The wooden stockade that surrounded the village rotted and had to be replaced about every ten years. During the 1740s when the palisade needed replacement, the old walls were left in place and a new stockade was erected six or seven feet beyond. The space between the new walls and the old was called the *Chemin de ronde*, where sentries walked their beat. This was the fort that Michel Chartier de Lotbinière saw in 1749 when the Governor of Canada sent him to draw a plan of Michilimackinac and prepare a report. A trained engineer, the twenty-six-year-old Lotbinière was not impressed by the rude fort with its twelve-foot-high walls. The fort was not quite square, with sides measuring from 301 to 338 feet. Small bastions were located on each corner, and sentry boxes stood on the southeast and northwest bastions. Two strong oak gates provided entrance into the fortified town. A single gate opened on the water side and a double door faced the land.

Inside the fort was an open space called the *Place D'Armes* where the thirty soldiers paraded for drill. The garrison was changed every three years, but the soldiers could remain if they wished. Several chose to do so; some had served for more than twenty years. The opportu-

Colonial Michilimackinac **39**

ABOVE: Interior of reconstructed powder magazine: notice the original floorboards and remains of the log wall. BELOW: French outdoor bake oven OPPOSITE: Fish were preserved by smoking.

nity to do a little fur trading made their decision worthwhile. In the center of the parade ground was a *Calvaire*, or large crucifix. Facing on the parade ground was the home of Commandant François Lefebvre Duplessis Faber, the church, the priest's house, the guard house, the sergeant's house, and the junior officers' house. Also facing the open space were houses owned by over twenty traders. In all there were forty houses, most of which were twenty-three feet square and were built by placing upright poles in trenches dug in the ground. The spaces between the logs were caulked inside and out with clay. Cedar bark covered the roofs. Because the house poles rotted quickly, some of the houses had to be propped up. A few buildings, including the church, were constructed from squared timbers and had board roofs. Tucked away in the southeast corner of the fort was a semi-subterranean powder magazine whose roof was covered with sod to protect it against fire. The fort was defended by four small cannons, which fired half-pound iron balls, and a small mortar, which fired a hollow iron exploding shell four inches in diameter and marked by a French fleur de lys.

Outside the fort walls were three dome-shaped French-style bake ovens and an ice house. There were also stables for the animals belonging to Augustin Langlade, the prominent trader who was the husband of an Odawa woman and the father of Charles, the military officer. The Langlades lived at Michilimackinac for many years. The fort sat on a sandy beach and the sand had blown up into sand hills around the fort. Winds from the west, north, and east hit the exposed fort with full force. Loose sand blew into the houses during the summer and snow found its way through the cracks in the winter.

Only ten French families resided at Michilimackinac year-round; three of them were Métis. Though they planted small gardens and did some fishing and hunting, they also purchased fish and wild game, including deer and moose, and the primary item in their diet – corn – from the Indians. Without the food obtained from the nearby Native peoples, the French at Michilimackinac would have starved. A few domestic animals were raised: in 1749 at Michilimackinac there were three cows, one bull, four horses, fifty or sixty chickens, and seven or eight pigs. These were scarcely enough to provide food for the community.

Maple sugar was also an important food. The French learned from the Native peoples how to tap nearby maple trees each spring when the sap began to flow. Temporary camps were set up in the maple groves while families boiled down the sap to make syrup and maple sugar. Sugar is very nutritious and does not spoil. It also makes corn mush taste much better.

Preserving food was always a problem. Corn and sugar would last indefinitely if kept dry. Meat and fish were smoked or salted. During the winter, meat was preserved simply by keeping it cold, and people cut ice from the frozen lake and stored it in an insulated icehouse to provide a limited amount of cooling in the summer. Most residents dug small storage cellars beneath the floors of their houses, where certain foods stayed cool and could be kept for extended periods of time.

Meals were cooked in open fireplaces. Food preparations took a lot of time even with the help of slaves and children. Corn had to be pounded to make meal or flour, and kettles had to be watched and stirred as they boiled and simmered over the fire. Pies and

BELOW: The French dug this well to provide a secure water source in case of attack. Perhaps it was dug in 1747 when Michilimackinac was threatened by hostile Indians. OPPOSITE: The fireplace was the center of the home. Here meals were cooked and the family gathered around on cold winter days.

cakes were baked in Dutch ovens buried in the coals on the hearth. Bread was usually baked in the large ovens outside the fort. Fires were built in the ovens to heat them up; then the coals were raked out and the dough placed inside. Soon the delicious aroma signaled that the fresh bread was nearly ready. Since it took a lot of work to prepare the oven, baking was not done every day. The simple meals were enhanced with coffee, tea, and chocolate brought from Montreal. Tobacco was also imported because smoking helped the men pass the time. Some of the men had been *voyageurs* and remembered taking a regular break from paddling to smoke a pipe. A little brandy also helped settle stomachs after a meal.

Both the Native peoples and the French owned dogs. Dogs were more than pets; they were frequently used to pull small sleds during the winter. When the lakes froze, canoes were useless but dog sleds could go swiftly over the ice and snow. Dogs even helped haul the massive amounts of fire-wood needed to keep the Michilimackinac residents warm in winter.

The winters were long and cold at Michilimackinac and the residents

had to do a great deal of work simply to stay warm. They needed fifteen cords of wood (a pile four feet wide, four feet high, and 120 feet long) to keep each fireplace burning. By the 1740s people had to go more than a mile from the fort to cut firewood and it took a lot of hauling to get it home. Much of the time in the winter was spent just keeping warm.

There was still time for fun. A few of the residents knew how to play the fiddle, and their music enlivened many an evening as people pushed the furniture back against the walls to make room to dance. Sometimes the family gathered around the flickering fire and listened to frightening tales of the *Loup-garou* (Werewolf).

Weddings were celebrated with music, dancing, and food. On a cold winter day in February 1747, Pierre Pelletier from Montreal married Françoise Parent, daughter of Pierre Parent and Marie Anne Chaboillez, who resided at Michilimackinac. Father Pierre Du Jaunay presided at the ceremony and family and friends joined in the celebration.

Many festivities centered around the church. Christmas was a major religious feast. Early in December, animals were slaughtered to provide food for the occasion. Special foods were prepared and fat was saved from the animals to make candles. Candles lit up the houses and the church in the days before Christmas. A lot of candles were needed for the Midnight

Mass on Christmas Eve. The church bell summoned all to attend. It was a spectacular sight with all the candles burning and a decorated crèche, or manger scene. People raised their voices in song and the priest celebrated three Masses. Leaving the cold church, everyone returned home for a sumptuous meal called the *réveillon*. Following the meal, singing, dancing, jigging, and storytelling went on until sunrise.

Another big party took place on New Year's Day. Everyone went to church in the morning and greeted each other by shaking hands and kissing. Then families gathered in their homes to receive a blessing from the oldest man. Later, men dressed in their best clothes and went to neighbors' homes, where the lady of the house would invite the men in to visit. Inside, they exchanged greetings and kisses with all the girls. After a drink of brandy and a few snacks, the men went on to the next house. New Year's was also the day for gift-giving, though gifts were modest. A few days later, at Epiphany, the "Feast of the Three Kings," a special cake was baked with a bean inside. The person who found the bean became king or queen for the day and everyone had to obey the royal commands. The day was devoted to fun, dancing, and games. The Christian Odawa at St. Ignace mission also observed these customs.

Although life at Michilimackinac was difficult, the people managed to create comfort and normalcy in their days. The settlement was expanding, however, and conflicts abroad would soon bring violence and change to the Straits.

OPPOSITE: Ice locked Michilimackinac in its frozen grip and isolated the community for several months each year. ABOVE: Decorated wine glass LEFT: Brass finger rings were common trade items.

OPPOSITE: Red-coated British soldiers prepare to fire their flintlock muskets. RIGHT: Brass French military button from a soldier at Michilimackinac.

Imperial Conflicts

DURING THE EIGHTEENTH CENTURY, the two major European powers – England and France – fought for dominance. The question of who should sit on the thrones of these countries led to wars that reverberated around the world. Both France and England were actively extending their power by creating and capturing overseas colonies. North America became a battleground in a series of wars and Michilimackinac was not exempt from the conflicts. During this period, war was more normal than peace. North America witnessed King William's War 1689-1697; Queen Anne's War 1702-1713; King George's War 1740-1748; and the French and Indian War 1754-1760. The longest period of peace was the twenty-seven years from 1713 to 1740, when the settlement of Michilimackinac was expanding.

During the first half of the eighteenth century, the English who were living hundreds of miles to the north and east of Michilimackinac were not much of a problem for the French settled there, but by mid-century the English had become a threat. Only 10,000 French people had immigrated to North America. Canada's population grew primarily through natural increase from the large Catholic families. The English colonies, however, received hundreds of thousands of immigrants, mostly farmers seeking new lands. By the mid-eighteenth century English frontier farmers were pushing westward into Pennsylvania and Virginia, and northward into New York. British traders were also taking pack horses over the Appalachian Mountains into the Ohio country. Allied with the Iroquois and Delaware, they built trading relationships with the Ohio tribes, including the Huron, who were led by Nicholas, and the Miami, led by

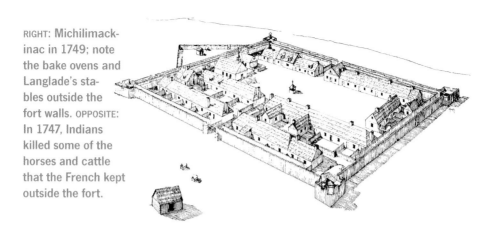

RIGHT: **Michilimack-inac in 1749; note the bake ovens and Langlade's sta-bles outside the fort walls.** OPPOSITE: **In 1747, Indians killed some of the horses and cattle that the French kept outside the fort.**

Memeskia, called "La Demoiselle."

In time of war, the French felt that the best defense against their more populous enemy was a good offense. Because the French population was very small, they relied heavily on Native allies. In 1745, Commandant Louis de la Corne recruited sixty Odawa and Ojibwa to follow Charles-Joseph Noyelles, Jr. to attack Saratoga, New York. The French employed guerilla tactics and launched a series of swift hit-and-run raids against out-lying farms or small settlements. Directed by a few French officers, some of whom were related to the tribesmen, such as Charles Langlade, the war parties were composed primarily of Indian warriors. Many young Native men were eager to go on a raid, since success on the war path was one of the primary ways they achieved status among their band. Each warrior decided for himself if he wanted to join a particular party. The French supplied guns, ammunition, clothing, and food, as well as providing for the women and children during their men's absence.

The Michilimackinac Odawa continued to support the French, but not all the western tribes were friendly. By the late 1740s the Huron, encouraged by English traders, had became hostile to the French and stirred up some of the Odawa at Saginaw Bay and some of the Ojibwa at Mackinac. In the summer of 1747, the garrison at Michilimackinac was threatened by several violent Indian actions. Charles-Joseph Noyelles, Jr., commanding at the post in the absence of Louis de la Corne, learned that three traders on their way from Detroit to Michilimackinac were killed by the Saginaw Odawa. Two canoes full of traders were also attacked north of Manitoulin

Island in Lake Huron. On Mackinac Island a trader was stabbed by some Ojibwa warriors. The same Indians killed horses and cattle outside Michilimackinac's stockade and, at a council held on July 3, made plans to surprise the garrison. The plot was discovered and the soldiers were alerted by the ringing of the church bell and the beating of "tap too" on the drum. Armed sentries locked the gates and prevented any Indian from entering the fort. Rumors were rife that a grand plot to eliminate the French had been hatched and that even the Odawa at L'Arbre Croche were involved. As a precaution, all the traders who had gathered at Michilimackinac for the summer rendezvous were detained until the situation quieted down.

When word of the trouble reached Montreal, a relief expedition of ten canoes was organized and dispatched under the command of Jacques Legardeur de Saint-Pierre. Meanwhile thirty-three canoes loaded with furs set off from the Straits for Montreal. They encountered five canoes with hostile Natives but drove them off. When Saint-Pierre arrived at Michilimackinac after a forty-five-day journey, he seized all the merchandise, detained the *voyageurs*, and threatened to prevent any traders from going out unless the murderers were turned in and the plunder returned. Saint-Pierre's firmness met with success. One murderer was brought in from Sagi-

naw and another from the Michilimackinac area, and two hostages were given in place of the murderers who were not apprehended. The Indians even returned a portion of the plunder and agreed to pay for the remainder. The murderers were placed under guard in a canoe and taken to Montreal for trial and possible execution.

Peace returned to Michilimackinac, but hundreds of miles to the east, between Montreal and Quebec, an amazing drama played out as described in a letter at the time: "Mr. De Longueuil put the three prisoners safely and secretly on board one of the King's canoes, under the command of one of the best Sergeants of the garrison along with seven picked soldiers, and enjoined on them all the precautions requisite to be taken in such a case; but in vain. The negligence of the Sergeant cost him his life; those three men, without arms, and with manacles on their feet, killed or drowned eight well armed men, and having cut their irons with an axe on the bows of the canoe, escaped ashore and thence into the woods."

Charles Langlade, whose mother was an Odawa from L'Arbre Croche, emerged as a highly successful leader, often in partnership with his uncle La Fourche, an Odawa war chief. In 1752 during a lull in the Imperial war, Langlade, who was then twenty-three, led a party of three hundred to

Pickawillany, Ohio to oppose the English thrust into the Ohio country. The British traders were captured and the Miami chief Memeskia, "La Demoiselle," was boiled and eaten by the Odawa warriors. This practice was not uncommon among Native warriors, who believed that consuming the fallen body of a respected enemy would help them to gain his power.

A few years later in 1755, western warriors participated in the spectacular victory over British General Edward Braddock in western Pennsylvania near present-day Pittsburgh. Langlade and La Fourche were present at the capture of Fort William Henry in upstate New York in 1757 and the Odawa were involved in killing some of the surrendered British soldiers. When the Odawa warriors returned from this campaign, they carried with them the dreaded small pox. The horrid disease spread rapidly among both the French and Odawa at Michilimackinac, and Father Marin-Louis Le Franc recorded in the parish register the burial of many, both young and old.

Odawa warriors from Michilimackinac, led by Langlade, were on the Plains of Abraham at Quebec in 1759 when the superior British forces defeated the French army and seized control of the St. Lawrence River. Since all supplies to and from Canada passed up the river, it was only a matter of time before Montreal capitulated. When Canada surrendered, in 1760, Michilimackinac was included. A new era at the Straits had begun.

OPPOSITE: Odawa and other Native warriors were a vital part of the French fight against the British. BELOW: When the British captured Montreal, Michilimackinac was included in the surrender.

LEFT: This pewter button was worn by one of the British soldiers of the 60th Regiment who occupied Michilimackinac in 1761. OPPOSITE: Soldiers spent a great deal of time culling firewood for the long Michilimackinac winters.

Redcoats at the Straits

THE CAPITULATION OF CANADA on September 8, 1760 provided that the French soldiers were to surrender their arms, people's property rights were to be respected, and the Catholic faith was to be permitted. The capitulation applied only to Canada and not to Louisiana, which was also part of New France in North America. The dividing line between the two provinces was in the middle of Illinois. Furthermore, the war between England and France was not over. It raged until the Peace of Paris in 1763.

At Michilimackinac, Commandant Louis Liénard de Beaujeu et de Villemonde refused to comply with the terms of capitulation. Instead of waiting for English soldiers to arrive and surrendering to them, Beaujeu readied his soldiers for a harsh winter trip southward to the Louisiana colony so that they could continue to fight. Beaujeu left Charles Langlade in charge of the fort and the remaining French traders and their families.

The Odawa and Ojibwa were confused and infuriated. They had not been defeated in battle and had not been consulted about the capitulation. As independent people, they still considered the English their enemies.

Soon after the capture of Montreal, the British Army dispatched a swiftly moving force, led by Robert Rogers of the Rangers, to secure the surrender of Detroit. Only about 1,500 French lived permanently in the upper Great Lakes, including Detroit, Michilimackinac, Fort St. Joseph, Sault Ste. Marie, and Green Bay. However, more than 10,000 Native peoples lived in the region. The expedition to Detroit was successful, but when the English attempted to go north to Michilimackinac, winter storms forced them to return. But the Straits had not seen the last of Rogers. He would return as Commandant with grand dreams and a role to

play in Michilimackinac's dramatic history.

A number of British traders had accompanied the soldiers to Detroit and some made plans to travel to Michilimackinac as soon as possible. They knew that because the French had not been able to export furs to France for several years, there must be a large amount of furs waiting at Michilimackinac to be traded.

Eager British traders moved faster than the army. Alexander Henry, Henry Bostwick, and a few others went to Montreal, obtained permission to go to Michilimackinac, hired canoemen, and purchased merchandise. They teamed up with French traders who knew the route and how to outfit a brigade. As soon as all was ready, they embarked up the Ottawa River for the interior. The year was 1761. Twenty-two-year-old Alexander Henry, who had been born in the British colony of New Jersey, was in the lead. As the canoes reached Lake Huron, they encountered Native peoples who eyed Henry distrustfully because his English clothes identified his nationality. Quickly he changed into French clothing to avoid detection.

ABOVE: Alexander Henry was the first British trader to reach Michilimackinac. He later wrote a book about his adventures. OPPOSITE: British creamware platter and a Chinese porcelain teacup used by the residents of Michilimackinac.

On Mackinac Island, the party stopped briefly (as was the custom) to clean themselves before arriving at Michilimackinac.

The Ojibwa who were camped there became suspicious of Henry and he became very nervous.

Arriving at Michilimackinac, Henry's associate Étienne Campion pretended to be in charge. However, the residents of Michilimackinac soon realized that a despised Englishman had come into their midst. Some feared that they would lose their trading business to the English.

Others, like François Louis Cardin, had previously served as soldiers in the French garrison. They had settled at Michilimackinac after years of resisting their English enemies, and the old hatreds still burned. People gathered around Henry and tried to frighten him into fleeing to Detroit. They informed him that the whole Ojibwa band from Mackinac Island was coming to see him. Henry felt very alone.

Post interpreter Jacques Philippe Farley, married to an Ojibwa woman, was summoned to help. Farley explained to Henry the customs of the country. He said that when a stranger arrives it is customary for the chiefs to come to greet him. They give the stranger a small gift and expect a gift in return. Because Henry was English, the chiefs would expect a large gift. Farley was concerned because the Ojibwa boasted that they would not permit any Englishmen to come among them.

The arriving Ojibwa were a frightening sight.

Sixty warriors, led by six-foot-tall chief Minavavana, walked in single file, each carrying a tomahawk and a scalping knife. Their faces were painted with charcoal and their naked upper bodies were decorated with patterns of white clay. Some had feathers sticking through their noses or in their hair. The Ojibwa filed into the room and seated themselves on the floor.

After smoking the pipes, Minavavana, who was much taller than Henry, rose to speak: "Englishman, you know that the French king is our father . . . You are his enemy; and how, then, could you have the boldness to venture among us, his children? You know that his enemies are ours . . . Englishman, although you have conquered the French, you have not conquered us! We are not your slaves . . . Englishman, your king has never sent us any presents, nor entered into any treaty with us, wherefore he and we are still at war . . . But, for you, we have taken into consideration, that you have ventured your life among us, in the expectation that we should not molest you. You do not come armed, with an intention to make war; you come in peace, to trade with us, and supply us with necessaries, of which we are in much want. We shall regard you, therefore, as a brother; and you may sleep tranquilly, without fear of the Chipeways. As a token of our friendship, we present you with this pipe, to smoke." A pipe was presented to Henry to smoke. After he puffed three times, it was given to the chief and then to everybody in the room.

At the end of the ceremony, Minavavana requested that his young men be allowed to taste some English "milk," meaning rum. Henry prom- ised to give them a small cask at the time of their leaving. Speaking through the inter- preter Farley, Henry told the Ojibwa that the French king had sur-

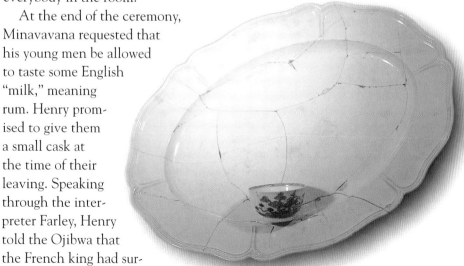

rendered Canada to the King of England, who would now serve as a father and take good care of them. The Indians gave their approval and Henry distributed presents and a small amount of rum. He was relieved that the Ojibwa were satisfied. But he had forgotten about the Odawa.

Upon hearing that English traders had arrived at Michilimackinac, the Odawa chief La Fourche and some of his people decided to go to see for themselves. Several other traders, including Henry Bostwick, James Stanley Goddard, and Ezekiel Solomon, had arrived at Michilimackinac a few days after Henry. Two hundred Odawa warriors came into the fort and stayed in the houses of their French relatives and friends. The next day they gathered formally in the former Commandant's house and summoned the English traders. The Odawa told the traders that they wanted a large quantity of trade goods to be given to them on credit.

Perplexed, the traders asked for a day to decide what to do. When Jacques Farley indicated that the Odawa planned to kill them, the traders gathered thirty of their men into a house and armed themselves against an attack. The next day the English told the Odawa that they would not meet their terms. Someone had told the traders that English soldiers were only five miles away and would arrive in the morning. The night was anxious for both the British traders and the Odawa, who held a midnight council. After consulting with the fort's inhabitants, the Odawa decided not to confront the British military and drifted out of the fort.

At noon on September 28, 1761, a column of soldiers of the British 60th Regiment marched into Michilimackinac with Captain Henry Balfour of the

BELOW: Brass serpent sideplate from a British flintlock trade musket
OPPOSITE: British soldiers drill on the parade ground at Michilimackinac.

80th Regiment in command. It had taken the British Army all summer to obtain adequate provisions and organize a force to send into Lakes Huron and Michigan to occupy the French forts. Twenty-eight red-coated soldiers remained at Michilimackinac under the command of Lieutenant William Leslye. The rest of the troops paddled *bateaux* along the north shore of Lake Michigan to Green Bay. They then followed the west shore of Lake Michigan south past the Chicago River and up the east shore to the St. Joseph River. Engineer Dietrich Brehm, who was with the expedition, drew the first English map of the area.

The English settled in to stay. Lieutenant Leslye occupied the former Commandant's house and quartered his soldiers in the buildings where French soldiers had formerly lived. A group of Odawa and Ojibwa came to

ABOVE: British soldiers traded with the local merchants and occasionally also with the Native people.

OPPOSITE TOP: Silver earring used in the Indian trade

OPPOSITE BOTTOM: This fragment of a brass hoop from a powder barrel was marked with the King's Broad Arrow to indicate it belonged to the British government.

pay formal respect to the new Commandant. The traders dispatched canoe loads of merchandise to the west and north. Some traders returned to Montreal but Alexander Henry and some others stayed for the winter.

The winter of 1761 was a time of adjustment for the British soldiers as well as for the French inhabitants. The soldiers remained aloof from local people, though some were attracted by the young women. The English were all Protestants. The Church of England was the official religion, with the king as its head. Catholicism was outlawed in England and was permitted in Canada only as part of its capitulation. The soldiers thought that the Catholics were incredibly superstitious or slaves of the Pope. Consequently, the English did not attend any of the Catholic church ceremonies. On the other hand, the French Catholics regarded the British as heretics who were outside the pale of the church.

Language was a major barrier to communications.

A few English traders knew a little French, but none knew any of the Native languages. Though they distrusted the interpreter Farley, they had to employ him when they spoke with the Odawa and Ojibwa.

Everybody was pleased that trade had resumed. The stockpile of furs had been sent to Montreal for sale and the supplies of gunpowder, cloth, and alcohol had been refurbished. The French had always traded brandy, which is distilled from grapes, whereas the English used rum distilled from sugar cane grown on their West Indian Island colonies.

As their need for trade overcame their initial distrust, the Odawa brought corn to trade with the English. Food was expensive and in short supply. Father Du Jaunay slaughtered an ox and sold the meat at a high price. The traders and some of the military supplemented their diet by hunting and fishing. Fish, caught by hook and line through the ice, were abundant and provided a large part of the diet of the civilians. The change in diet was difficult for the British soldiers, who were used to eating salt beef.

During the summer of 1762, thirty-year-old Captain George Etherington arrived to assume command of Michilimackinac. He divided his command and sent German-born Lieutenant John Jamet with a detachment of soldiers to garrison the small fort at Sault Ste. Marie, fifty miles to the north. Etherington and Jamet and their soldiers settled into life at the Straits, confident in their country's victory. They little dreamed that this superior attitude would soon be their undoing.

OPPOSITE: Ojibwa Indians rush into the open gate of Fort Michilimackinac after over-powering the sentries and officers June 2, 1763. BELOW: British soldiers line up for inspection.

Pontiac's Uprising

IN 1763 THE WAR in Europe between France and England still raged. In North America British soldiers were wary of the French and their Indian relatives and friends. The English government was trying to save money. Now that the French military in Canada had been defeated, the British could see no reason to continue passing out expensive presents to Native peoples, particularly those who had been enemies. British officers con-temptuously looked down on the tribesmen, whom they considered uncivi-lized and only a step up from animals. It seemed unnecessary to follow these people's customs of giving regular gifts as expressions of friendship. Furthermore, it made no sense to sell gunpowder and muskets to former enemies while war was still going on. Consequently, Lieutenant Leslye and Captain Etherington had very few presents for visiting tribesmen and they prohibited traders from taking gunpowder into the interior.

The Odawa and Ojibwa viewed the situation differently. They sensed

that the British soldiers did not respect them. The French Commandant had understood and respected their customs, but the new Commandant was differ-ent. The English father was not nearly as generous as their French father and the absence of presents showed a lack of love. Not

only were the British unfriendly but they appeared to be actively trying to harm the Native people. Odawa and Ojibwa hunters relied on muskets to hunt animals for hides and food. Without gunpowder it was much more difficult to kill a bear, elk, or deer. Without meat their wives and children would be hungry and might even starve. Did the English father not care about them? Perhaps the French father was only sleeping and would return. Their French friends and relatives suggested that this might be so. The French were not far away because the white French flag still flew in the Illinois Country.

Word spread among the tribes that the Master of Life was not happy with the Native peoples because they had become too dependent upon things from across the distant sea. The words of Neolin the Delaware Prophet were passed from campfire to campfire. Wampum belts circulated suggesting an uprising against the arrogant redcoats. Some welcomed the idea; others opposed it. On May 9th, Odawa Chief Pontiac led an assault on Detroit. Word of the uprising soon reached the Natives at the Straits, but the English soldiers did not hear about it. At Michilimackinac, the Ojibwa wanted to attack. Minavavana, known as the Grand Saulteur, harbored deep resentments against the British. Over fifty years old and no

longer vigorous, he found a willing listener in young Matchekewis. Together they devised a plan to rid themselves of the redcoats. Skilled warriors, they valued stealth, cunning, and surprise. They thought that the white men were foolish to stand in the open in long lines and shoot at each other. Too many of one's own people were killed fighting that way. Far better to stalk your enemy carefully and fall upon him when he least expects it. Strike hard and fast and then fade away if the enemy is too strong. The Ojibwa knew how to use their guns but they were also skilled with knife and tomahawk. These weapons were easily concealed, made no noise, and were very effective in close combat.

The English at Michilimackinac had a few cannons, and each soldier carried a musket to which he could attach a long, sharp bayonet. The fort was enclosed by a stout twelve-foot-high palisade wall. Sentries guarded the gates and opened them only in the daytime. However, the thirty-five soldiers of the fort garrison could be easily surprised and overcome. If a large number of warriors could be assembled near the open gate, they could overpower the unsuspecting garrison. A game of *baggatiway* lacrosse would be an ideal cover for assembling a large group of warriors. The presence of some visiting Sac from the West provided a good reason for the game, and the open field near the fort's land gate would be an excellent place to play. Unaware of the assault in Detroit, the English soldiers would not be suspicious of such a gathering.

During the night of Wednesday, June 1, 1763 Minavavana and Matchekewis laid out their plans. Women were instructed to gather near the gate to watch the game. Beneath their blankets they carried knives and tomahawks. They invited Captain Etherington to come out of the fort to watch the sport and encouraged him to wager on an Ojibwa victory. Lieutenant John Jamet, having returned from garrisoning the fort at Sault Ste. Marie, strolled out to watch the game, along with several off-duty soldiers.

During the height of the energetic game, at a prearranged signal, the ball was thrown over the wall of the fort and the players rushed to retrieve it. Women standing by the open gate handed them knives and tomahawks as they passed. The sentries at the gate were immediately cut down as warriors swarmed into the fort. Only Lieutenant Jamet resisted. Drawing his sword, he fought against five assailants before they knocked him down with multiple wounds. Warriors killed fifteen soldiers in the first rush and captured the rest. Some soldiers tried to escape or hide but they were quickly found. An English trader named Mr. Tracey was killed at the lakeside as he greeted an incoming canoe full of traders. The Natives feared that the new arrivals might bring word of Pontiac's uprising to Michilimackinac, and they

OPPOSITE: The Ojibwa carefully planned their successful attack on the unsuspecting British garrison. BELOW: Knives such as these, excavated at Michilimackinac, were used by the Ojibwa to capture the fort.

would not take that chance. Henry Bostwick and Ezekiel Solomon were taken prisoner. Alexander Henry hid for a night in Charles Langlade's loft, but he was finally turned over to the Indians by the frightened family.

The French residents were surprised and shocked but did not dare help the British soldiers. Most had no attachment to their former enemies. The Ojibwa directed their fury against the British and did not molest the French. Some British soldiers were separated from the others and five were eventually killed. The surviving British feared for their lives. Father Du Jaunay, appalled by the slaughter, opened his house to the British captives and protected them.

The Odawa at L'Arbre Croche had not participated in the attack. A day or two later La Fourche and a large number of Odawa warriors came to Michilimackinac and berated the Ojibwa for attacking without consulting them. They demanded all the prisoners and a share of the loot. The Ojibwa protested, but the more numerous Odawa had their way. The Odawa, long experienced as traders, realized that it was better to support rather than oppose the British. They knew that the British controlled the fur trade routes and the flow of merchandise to the Great Lakes Country. All the surviving British soldiers and merchants were turned over to the Odawa, except Alexander Henry, who remained a prisoner of the Ojibwa chief Wawatam, who safeguarded the Englishman. As other unsuspecting traders arrived from the East with canoes laden with trade goods, the Odawa took them under their protection.

In order to protect the British, the Odawa took the soldiers to L'Arbre Croche. Charles Langlade, now in charge of the fort again, became the focal point of authority in the chaotic situation. Captain Etherington purchased trade goods from the British merchants and gave them to the Odawa to ensure their continuing support. To inform the authorities about the capture of Michilimackinac, Etherington dispatched Father Du Jaunay to Detroit. Detroit was under siege from Pontiac's warriors, but Etherington was certain that Du Jaunay could get through the Indian lines because

OPPOSITE: Axes were easily concealed but were deadly in battle. LEFT: Captain George Etherington wrote to Lieutenant James Gorrell at Green Bay telling him about the capture of the fort.

they respected him. In order to consolidate the scattered British forces in the Upper Lakes, Etherington sent word to Lieutenant James Gorrell at Green Bay to bring all his soldiers to L'Arbre Croche. It was too late to do anything for Fort St. Joseph to the south, which had been swiftly captured on May 25th and all the British killed or taken prisoner. Etherington waited at L'Arbre Croche until July, when Gorrell and his soldiers arrived. Then the Odawa escorted the British soldiers to Montreal by way of the Lake Nipissing/Ottawa River route, avoiding the conflict at Detroit.

The French inhabitants at Michilimackinac had mixed reactions to the situation. Some used the opportunity to loot merchandise from the British merchants' stores. Others carefully protected the merchandise, expecting that the British would return. Charles Langlade remained at the fort for several months, but moved, with his wife Charlotte and their two young daughters, to Green Bay the next year. When he left, Langlade turned over his position of authority at Michilimackinac to old Pierre Parent.

It was more than a year before British soldiers returned to Michilimackinac. During the summer of 1764, a few British merchants arrived but the redcoats did not reappear until September, when they were led by Captain William Howard. During the summer of 1764, the British Army, under

ABOVE: **When the British army returned in 1764, they were much more respectful to the Native people.** OPPOSITE: **Michilimackinac from the water**

Colonel John Bradstreet, attempted to pacify the western Native peoples. Sir William Johnson held an impressive conference at Niagara with the western tribes in an effort to gain their support, which succeeded. The triumph of the Indian uprising of 1763 had given the British authorities a rude shock. Forts at Green Bay, Michilimackinac, St. Joseph, Miami, Ouiatenon, Sandusky, Presqu' Isle, Le Boeuf, and Venango had been captured or abandoned. Forts Detroit, Pittsburgh, and Niagara were besieged. The Indians stopped fighting but were never defeated. The warriors had demonstrated their power and thus earned the begrudging respect of British authorities. Finally, with the aid of British sailing vessels, the siege at Detroit was relieved.

The British realized that the support and friendship of the Native peoples was essential if their small garrisons were to survive and if the profitable trade was to continue. The fur trade had collapsed with the uprising in 1763. Only with peace could the trade resume. The British recognized that to gain and maintain the support of the tribes it was necessary to provide presents on a regular basis. These tokens of good will were essential to cordial relationships. British Commandants at Michilimackinac learned to treat the Native peoples with new respect.

During the years immediately after 1764, British authorities struggled to find the best way to regulate the Indian trade. Some felt that the trade should be tightly regulated and permitted only in a few locations where British authorities could supervise. This had been the pattern in the colony of New York, where the Indian trade had been limited to Albany and later Oswego. Some now wanted to limit the trade to Michilimackinac, Detroit, Niagara, Pittsburgh, and perhaps a few other places. The Indians would have to carry their furs to these few locations to trade.

Others favored the French system, which licensed traders to take merchandise directly to the Indian villages. By the late 1760s, the British had worked out a trade policy. Traders would be permitted to take merchandise into the interior, but they had to obtain passes to transport approved amounts of merchandise to specific points. The Commandant at Michilimackinac was responsible to check the passes of the merchants who came to or traveled through the Straits.

In 1763, the war between England and France had finally been settled. At the Treaty of Paris, all of New France, including Louisiana, was turned over to Great Britain. The French lands west of the Mississippi were ceded to Spain. Now the French Canadians knew for certain that if they wanted to remain in their homes they must make accommodation with British authorities. There was no longer a hope that the French government would return. In the Illinois Country, some of the French who did not want to live under the British king moved west across the Mississippi and founded a new community at St. Louis. However, at Michilimackinac, most of the French inhabitants remained.

OPPOSITE: When the British returned in 1764, they enlarged the fort and kept careful watch at the gates. RIGHT: Pewter button of a 10th Regiment soldier

The British Settle In

IN THE YEARS FOLLOWING the Indian uprising, Michilimackinac experienced strong economic growth. Because trade had stagnated for several years, the Native peoples needed trade goods and had bales of furs to trade. British traders flocked to Michilimackinac. Many followed the old French route from Montreal up the Ottawa River. Others came from New York by way of Albany, the Mohawk River, Oswego, Niagara, and Detroit. The advantage of the latter route was that the British had built sailing vessels to carry freight on Lakes Ontario and Erie. The ships had proven indispensable in relieving the siege of Detroit. In 1764 Captain Patrick Sinclair sailed up the St. Clair River to Lake Huron and then on to Michilimackinac with British soldiers who were to re-garrison the fort. When the *Gladwin* sailed into view at Michilimackinac, it opened up whole new possibilities for trade at the Straits.

No longer would everything that came to Michilimackinac have to be carried on the backs of *voyageurs*, lugged step by step over thirty-six *portages*. Now large, heavy items could be loaded on sailing ships at Fort Erie not far from Niagara and transported directly to Michilimackinac. The canny twenty-eight-year-old Scot who captained the *Gladwin* was impressed by the possibilities at the Straits, and also noted certain difficulties. For instance, the waters off Michilimackinac were shallow for several hundred yards out into the lake. This was no prob-

lem for *voyageurs* in canoes, but the larger sailing vessels had to off-load everything into small boats that were rowed to shore. A good harbor would make sailing much easier. During subsequent trips to Mackinac, Sinclair pondered the problem and fifteen years later was in a position to do something about it.

The British traders came to Mackinac from a variety of backgrounds. Alexander Henry was born in the colony of New Jersey; John Porteous came from Scotland; John Askin was from northern Ireland; and Ezekiel Solomon, a Jew born in Berlin, had moved to England and then to Canada. Some, like Nicolo Bezzo, had Italian names; Stephanus Groesbeck's ancestors were from the Netherlands. British traders spoke with many different accents and came from different cultural traditions, but they all understood the value of a shilling and worked hard to get it. The traders also knew that they needed the experience and skills of the French. Many British merchants formed partnerships with French traders and relied on the muscles of the French Canadian *voyageurs* to paddle their canoes. The crews on the sailing ships were also a mixed lot and included free Blacks and one Manuel Don Diago from Cuba.

There was some diversity, too, among the British soldiers who garrisoned the fort. They served in several regiments: 8th, 10th, 17th, and 60th. The soldiers were recruited primarily in England and Scotland, but the 60th "Royal Americans" enlisted a number of men from the colonies. The officers, who were changed every two years, included Frederick Spiesmacher, who spoke German.

A few soldiers and several officers

brought families
with them.
The soldiers
were quar-
tered in rental
houses, as
were most of
the officers.
After 1764 the
army stationed a larger con-
tingent of soldiers at Michilimackinac
to provide increased security. Instead of twenty
soldiers, which had been the normal French garrison,
the British now had fifty to seventy, and quarters
were cramped. The larger garrison changed the social
dynamics of Michilimackinac because soldiers and
civilians both lived inside the same stockade and
resided in adjacent housing.

Space was tight within the stockade. When the
rotting palisades needed rebuilding, their height was
increased to eighteen feet and the alignment was
changed on the north and south wall, so that the
extended walls could accommodate new military
buildings. To relieve the pressure for soldiers'
housing, Elias Smith, a carpenter from New York,
was brought to Michilimackinac in 1769 to construct
a log barracks to accommodate sixty soldiers.

When new traders came to Michilimackinac, they
had difficulty finding available houses inside the
stockade. The French had constructed a few houses
outside the walls. During the late 1760s Michilimackinac experienced a construction boom: over a
hundred houses were erected in these "suburbs" outside the stockade. Most of the houses were built
quickly and were intended only for summer use, but

ABOVE:
Michilimack-
inac as it looked
in the 1770s
OPPOSITE ABOVE: The
population of Michili-
mackinac expanded
rapidly after the
British returned.
OPPOSITE BELOW: Brass
shoe buckle found at
Michilimackinac

BELOW: Turlington's
Balsam of Life bottle
– a popular
medicine
OPPOSITE ABOVE:
Elizabeth Rogers
(*Reynolda House*)
OPPOSITE BELOW:
Jonathan Carver

at least one had a second story.

One of the merchants, twenty-five-year-old John Askin, who supplied food to the soldiers and the *voyageurs*, decided to try his hand at farming. In 1764 he acquired a half-interest in the Jesuit farm at L'Arbre Croche, and in 1774 Commandant Captain John Vattas granted him land for a farm at Three Mile Pond southwest of Michilimackinac. There Askin raised a variety of vegetables as well as pigs and cows. His farming was marginal but it added variety to his family's diet.

Michilimackinac, the westernmost outpost of the British empire, attracted visionaries and explorers, as it had done during the French regime. Explorers with limited geographical knowledge were drawn into the wilderness, dreaming of finding an all-water route across North America. Jean Nicollet had envisioned the route in the 1630s when he had tried to find Asia. Pierre Gaultier de La Vérendrye had searched for it in the 1730s and 1740s, but with limited success. Major Robert Rogers was also a man of dreams and action. Born in 1731 in Massachusetts, he rose to fame during the French and Indian War, leading a successful Ranger force against the French. In 1760 he was assigned the task of accepting the surrender of Detroit and Michilimackinac. Rogers rushed his men to Detroit and accepted its capitulation on November 29, but it was too late in the year to press on to Michilimackinac. However, the west had captured Rogers's imagination. In 1763 he returned again to Detroit to assist in raising the siege. While in London attempting to collect debts owed to him, he authored and published two books: *Journals of Major Robert Rogers* (London: 1765) and *A Concise Account of*

North America (London: 1765) which added to his fame. Fascinated by the untapped possibilities of the North American continent, Rogers secured an appointment as a Major in the 60th Regiment and as Commandant of Michilimackinac. To obtain these prestigious positions, he had gone over the heads of General Thomas Gage, the Commander of British Forces in North America, and Sir William Johnson, who was in charge of Indian Affairs and had successfully negotiated with the Natives at Niagara. These two resented Rogers's forwardness and warned their subordinates to keep a close eye on him.

Early in the summer of 1766, Rogers and his twenty-four-year-old wife, Elizabeth, the daughter of a New England minister, made their way west to Michilimackinac. Accompanying them were Jonathan Carver and Captain James Tute, whose mission was to lead an exploring expedition to the west. Wasting no time at Michilimackinac, Carver and Tute embarked in September. During the long winter months at the fort, Rogers consulted with many of the Mackinac traders and dreamed of creating a vast interior colony with himself as lieutenant governor. He formulated his ideas into a lengthy memo which he forwarded to England, but his dreams were not to be. During the summer Rogers had a serious quarrel with Benjamin Roberts, who had been appointed by Sir William Johnson to oversee Indian affairs. Then Tute and Carver returned without having found the northwest passage. Rogers was frustrated, but Carver went on to write and publish his account of the adventure, which became one of the eighteenth century's most popular travel books.

James Stanley Goddard, one of the first British traders at Michilimackinac, accompanied the exploring expedition of Tute and Carver.

Though the group did not explore any lands unknown to the French, they opened the eyes of English merchants to trade possibilities in the west and north. Rogers exceeded his authority and let a number of merchants carry merchandise west, angering those who did not enjoy the same privilege. In the years that followed, the west was officially opened to trade. Then British traders rapidly spread across the country, following in the footsteps of the French.

While Commandant at Michilimackinac, Rogers held many conferences with Indians who visited the fort. He listened attentively and provided presents to show his affection. Chief La Fourche and the L'Arbre Croche Odawa established a warm personal relationship with Rogers. During the French and Indian War, Rogers had fought both alongside and against Native warriors. He respected their skills and they respected him. Rogers reflected the changed English attitude toward the Native peoples after the 1763 uprising.

Rumors traveled eastward accusing Rogers of treasonous connections with the French. The charges were sufficient for General Gage to order the Commandant's arrest. On December 6, 1767, a file of soldiers arrested Rogers on the fort parade ground. All through the cold winter Rogers languished in irons. When La Fourche and his band returned in the spring from their winter hunting camps, they were very upset. The Ojibwa expressed their displeasure by throwing the British flag in the lake. When the ice released its grip, Rogers was thrown into the hold of the *Gladwin* and transported to Detroit. From there he was sent on to Niagara and then to Montreal for trial. Among the members at his General Court Martial trial in October 1768 were Captain George Etherington, who had commanded Michilimackinac in 1763, and Captain Arent Schuyler DePeyster, who would become Commandant in 1774. After a two-week trial, Rogers was found "Not Guilty" but he never returned to Michilimackinac.

Michilimackinac was the hub of the western fur trade for the English, as it had been for the French. At this major transshipment point merchandise flowed west and furs went east. Here food was provided for the *voyageurs*. Merchants such as John Askin purchased corn from Native peoples as far away as Milwaukee and from French farmers in the Detroit area and sold it to other traders and the soldiers.

Like the French before them, English traders formed alliances with Native women and often fathered children. Frequently such children were acknowledged and cared for, but all too often they were simply abandoned by their fathers. John Askin had three children, at least one of whom was Métis, before 1772, when he married Archange Barthe. Archange, who was from a well-connected French family in Detroit, was twenty-three years old when Askin

OPPOSITE: **Robert Rogers was highly respected by the Native peoples.** *(William L. Clements Library)*
ABOVE: **English pitcher found at Michilimackinac**
BELOW: **1766 map of Michilimackinac** *(William L. Clements Library)*

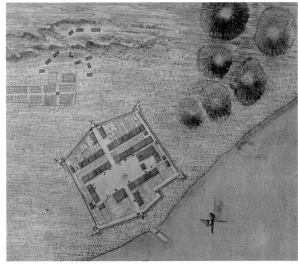

brought her to Michilimackinac to live with him and his children. He imported fine dresses for her to wear and had a sedan chair in which she could be carried.

Askin hired a number of employees and also owned two Black slaves, Pompey and Jupiter Wendell. It was common to give household slaves classical names. Jupiter's last name reflected his previous owner in Schenectady, New York. Jupiter was a skilled cooper and a valuable member of Askin's staff. Askin's Catholic marriage to Archange also cemented his relationship to the French community. Other British merchants, such as Ezekiel Solomon, married French Catholic wives, though Elizabeth Dubois Solomon remained in Montreal until late in her life.

John Askin, the wealthiest merchant at Michilimackinac, made part of his fortune by supplying food to the British soldiers. To facilitate his trade, Askin constructed several vessels, including the sloops *Welcome* and *Archange* and the schooner *Captain De Peyster*. He and his family socialized with the

British officers. They read the same books in French and English, drank tea from Chinese export porcelain cups, and ate their meals from English Wedgwood plates. Askin's friends referred to him as "Paddy," a nickname referring to his Irish background.

The French Catholic community suffered a severe blow when Father Du Jaunay left Michilimackinac in 1765 to return to Montreal. Nearly sixty years old, Du Jaunay had been an active part of the Michilimackinac community for almost thirty years and he was sorely missed. Laymen attended to the affairs of the church but priests such as Pierre Gibault passed through Michilimackinac only occasionally in 1768 and 1775. The church silver was taken to Detroit for safekeeping. The British soldiers used the church on Sunday for Divine Services and read from the Anglican *Book of Common Prayer*. There was no resident priest at Mackinac for many years, although on occasion the merchants, including Ezekiel Solomon, petitioned for a priest and pledged monies for his support. Michilimackinac society tended to be lawless and rowdy and the presence of a priest had given the community a moral tone which many residents missed.

OPPOSITE ABOVE: **Sentry stands watch at the fort guardhouse.** OPPOSITE BELOW: **Jupiter Wendell skillfully constructs a barrel.** ABOVE: **This Chinese porcelain saucer was used at Michilimackinac.**

LEFT: **Captain Arent Schuyler DePeyster** *(Burton Historical Collection)* BELOW: **Rebecca Blair DePeyster came to Michilimackinac with her husband in 1774.** *(Private Scottish Collection)* OPPOSITE: **Captain DePeyster was the highly respected Commandant at Michilimackinac for six years.**

The Revolution

IN JULY 1774, Captain Arent Schuyler DePeyster and two companies of the King's 8th Regiment arrived to garrison the post. DePeyster would serve at Michilimackinac longer than any other British Commandant. Accompanying him was his Scottish wife, Rebecca. They had no children, but Rebecca adored pets, including her chipmunk, "Tim." The DePeysters soon made friends with a wide range of the people at the Straits. They treated people with respect and were respected in turn. DePeyster would need all his diplomatic and personal skills to guide the upper Great Lakes during a major crisis.

Tensions were growing high between the English colonies and the mother country. In April 1775, conflict erupted at Lexington and Concord, Massachusetts and soon many colonists were in armed rebellion against the soldiers of the Crown. Michilimackinac was hundreds of miles away from the center of conflict but the ripples of war soon shook the society and economy at the Straits. American revolutionaries gained control in New York and were eager to spread the revolt to Canada. In November 1775, rebels captured Montreal and moved down the St. Lawrence River to attack Quebec. The St. Lawrence River was the major trade route for importing trade goods and exporting furs. With both New York and Montreal in rebel hands, the soldiers at Michilimackinac could not be supplied and the merchants could not conduct their business.

As soon as DePeyster arrived at Michilimackinac, he

held conferences with the Odawa, the Ojibwa, and the western tribes to continue building good will. DePeyster distributed generous presents to emphasize British concern for the Native peoples and ensure their loyalty in the brewing conflict. These efforts succeeded. During the years since 1763, an alliance had been forged between the British and the Odawa and Ojibwa as well as the French Canadian and Métis peoples of the upper Great Lakes. Everyone realized that the fur trade bound them together. The Native peoples also feared the numerous American farmers who were moving westward over the Appalachian Mountains and carving farmsteads out of Indian lands in Kentucky and Ohio.

In the summer of 1776, DePeyster organized La Fourche's Odawa warriors and other Indian allies to go east to assist the British forces. James Stanley Goddard, an English trader, recruited the Menominee in Wisconsin. Joseph Louis Ainse, a Métis native of Michilimackinac who served as interpreter, assembled a party of Odawa and Ojibwa. When the war party came together at Michilimackinac, DePeyster appointed Charles Langlade, who had formerly organized many expeditions against the British, to lead the warriors against the American rebels. But by the time Langlade arrived at Montreal, the American army had already been driven out and the route to the ocean was open.

The trade route was never threatened again and the fur trade prospered during the years of turmoil. Michilimackinac, though on the fringe of the conflict militarily, was a center for organizing Indian allies to fight against the Americans who proclaimed their Inde-

pendence from the King on July 4, 1776. Many young warriors were eager to test their courage and gain renown on the warpath. In 1777, warriors from Michilimackinac participated in General John Burgoyne's disastrous expedition and defeat at Saratoga, New York. During the next year warriors again paddled east to fight in Canada.

In the Ohio and Illinois Country, the Americans were on the offensive. Thousands of frontier families flooded into the rich lands of Kentucky and eyed the lush lands across the river in Ohio. An American Colonel, George Rogers Clark, had remarkable success in capturing the towns of Kaskaskia, Cahokia, and Vincennes in the Illinois Country. Inhabited primarily by people of French descent, the towns surrendered quickly, encouraged by word that France had signed an alliance with the fledgling United States. When Henry Hamilton, the British Lieutenant Governor at Detroit, led a force to recapture Vincennes, he himself was captured by Clark and sent as a prisoner to Williamsburg, Virginia.

Both Detroit and Michilimackinac were wide open to American attacks. The British were greatly concerned because some of the western tribes, such as the Potawatomi, Sac, and Fox, were siding with the Americans. DePeyster convened a major conference with the tribes, including the distant Sioux, and also dispatched a third of his eighty men south to Fort St. Joseph to try to block a rumored American attack. DePeyster purchased the sloop *Welcome* from John Askin so that he could have an armed vessel to patrol the lakes and bring in supplies.

During the summer of 1779, DePeyster received word that he was being transferred to Detroit to replace Henry Hamilton, who had been captured by the rebels. The Michilimackinac merchants, sad to see the DePeysters go, commissioned a magnificent silver punch bowl as a token of their affection. DePeyster's replacement was Lieutenant Governor Patrick Sinclair. Sinclair was not a stranger at Michilimackinac. In 1764 he had captained the first British sailing ship to reach the Straits and had been impressed by the area's possibilities. He had been dreaming of it ever since, and subsequently had sailed to Michilimackinac a number of times. In 1775, he was appointed Lieutenant Governor of Michilimackinac, but, due to the circumstances of war, it took him four years to arrive. Now he was finally in a position to enact some of his grand visions for Mackinac.

Sinclair was concerned about the vulnerability of the wooden stockade fort located on the sandy beach close to shore. Its walls provided defense against arrows and muskets, but would be quickly shattered by cannon fire. Also, Sinclair knew that there was no harbor for sailing vessels near the fort. The best harbor in the area was at Mackinac Island. The island's high bluffs overlooked the harbor and its limestone could be quarried to construct a fort capable of withstanding a cannon attack. As soon as Sinclair arrived at the Straits, he sailed to Mackinac Island to take a look, but he had already made up his mind. He was going to move the fort and the community to Mackinac Island.

Sinclair was an impatient man. He knew what he wanted to do and wasted no time in setting his plan in motion. Without waiting for official approval, he arranged to dismantle a house and transport it to the

OPPOSITE: This silver punch bowl was presented to A.S. DePeyster by the merchants of Michilimackinac when he left the post. BELOW: Lieutenant Governor Patrick Sinclair moved the fort and community to Mackinac Island.

ABOVE: By the 1770s, the Fox Indians had become allies of the British. OPPOSITE: A "piece of eight" coin cut from a Spanish dollar.

Island. Next, he ordered Ste. Anne's Church to be moved over the ice, believing that relocating the church would encourage the civilians to follow. While his soldiers were busy constructing a blockhouse and wharf on the Island, Sinclair was organizing his Native allies for an expedition against the Spanish town of St. Louis.

Believing that the best defense is a good offense, Sinclair sent a two-pronged attack to capture St. Louis and neutralize the American and Spanish threat from the west. Spain had recently joined the world-wide war against Great Britain and was actively making alliances with western tribes. An impressive force of over 750 warriors was organized, with Matchekewis, the Ojibwa who had led the capture of Michilimackinac in 1763, prominent among them. The Spanish learned that the expedition was coming and prepared a spirited defense. When the British force attacked on May 26, 1780, they were shocked by the Spanish resistance. Unable to overrun the town quickly, the force faded away and headed back to Mackinac. Sinclair had spent a vast sum purchasing presents for the expedition and now the effort had come to nothing.

Fearing an American counter-attack, Sinclair redoubled his efforts to move the garrison and community to Mackinac Island. Most of the traders were willing to relocate, especially when Sinclair gave them free land and lots in town on the Island. Some of the French residents decided to move to the north side of the Straits. There they laid out a number of French-style ribbon farms centered on the bay at old

St. Ignace. A few traders remained on the mainland at what was known as Old Mackinac. One of these men, a Scot named Robert Campbell, constructed a dam and sawmill on Mill Creek about three miles from the old fort. He shrewdly anticipated that there would be a great demand for sawn boards because of the new construction on Mackinac Island.

One family that did not move to the Island was John Askin's. John and Archange Askin had become very close friends of the DePeysters, with whom they socialized and shared books. Askin soon had a falling out with Lieutenant Governor Sinclair and decided to follow the DePeysters to Detroit, where Archange's family also lived. One couple who did move to the Island was the Scottish Doctor David Mitchell and his twenty-year-old Métis wife, Elizabeth Bertrand. Dr. Mitchell served as surgeon for the soldiers of the King's 8th garrison. At Michilimackinac he had met and married Elizabeth, whose father was a fur trader and whose mother was kin to the Odawa and Ojibwa in the Mackinac area. While the doctor attended to his medical affairs, Elizabeth traded furs. She did very well, due to her many connections through her relatives. The Mitchells prospered, and their family grew. When they moved to Mackinac Island, they were given not only a lot in the town on Market Street where they erected a large two-story house, but also a sizable tract of land, which they cultivated as a farm.

The move from Michilimackinac took nearly two years. Houses and buildings such as the soldiers' barracks and the guardhouse were dismantled and floated over to Mackinac Island on sailing vessels or rafts. Other buildings, such as the powder magazine, were burned to eliminate any possible use by an attacking American force. Apple trees were dug up and transplanted; new gardens were sown. A stockade was constructed around the town to provide protection. In the new community, the fort and soldiers were up on the bluff by themselves while the separate civilian community was scattered along the harbor.

From Fort to Park

WHEN THE SOLDIERS and most of the traders moved to Mackinac Island, only a few traders stayed behind. William Burnet and several others lived there occasionally during the summer. The buildings that were left at Michilimackinac decayed, collapsed, and rotted away. Windblown sand drifted over the site and covered the stone fireplaces, sometimes several feet deep. Plants and trees grew up over the abandoned fort site. Some of the buildings and stockades had been built of rot-resistant cedar; more than fifty years later, remnants of structures poked up through the sand. Seth Eastmen visited the site in the 1820s and painted a watercolor of the abandoned fort. The historian Francis Parkman, while doing research for his famous book *The Conspiracy of Pontiac*, visited the fort site in 1845 and recorded in his journal the outline of some of the buildings.

During the French and British occupation of the area, the local Odawa and Ojibwa had granted permission for the use of the land. When the Peace Treaty of 1783 was signed at the end of the American Revolution, it included the Straits of Mackinac within the boundaries of the United States. Again the local Odawa and Ojibwa chiefs were not consulted and they resisted the American takeover and participated in a number of stunning victories over the American army in the Ohio Country. The tide turned against the Native warriors when they were defeated in 1794 by the American General Anthony Wayne at the Battle of Fallen Timbers in northwest Ohio. The following year a treaty was signed at Greenville, Ohio in which the Indians ceded some lands to the United States. The old Ojibwa Chief Matchekewis participated in that treaty, which recognized a small amount of land on both the north and south sides of the Straits as a military reservation.

Later, the United States Government by treaty purchased additional lands from the Native peoples. In 1810, government surveyor Aaron Greeley came to the Straits to survey the private claims. At that time, William McGulpin claimed lands at the west side of the mainland military reservation, and Robert Campbell claimed a 640-acre tract on the east end along Mill Creek. In order for private claims to be approved, owners had to prove that they had occupied the land prior to 1796, when the United States finally took control of the area. During the 1830s and 1840s, after the 1836 Treaty of Washington, surveyors marked out the land in mile-square sections.

By the mid-nineteenth century the United States was undergoing a transportation revolution. Steam-powered railroads were rapidly being built and visionary people were taking a fresh look at the landscape. As lands in Michigan and Wisconsin were being cleared for farming and railroad tracks were linking farms to markets, Edger Conkling believed that the Straits of Mackinac had great potential. He felt that the south side of the Straits might one day develop as rapidly as Chicago. Conkling bought a sizable tract of land and in 1857 laid out a town, which he called "Mackinaw City." (Mackinaw was spelled differently to distinguish it from Mackinac Island, but both are pronounced the same way.) To accommodate future growth, he platted 150 wide boulevards and designated the site of Fort Michilimack-

OPPOSITE: **British War of 1812 soldier's hat-plate found at Mill Creek**

ABOVE: **By the mid-nineteenth century the site of Michili-mackinac was covered by drifting sand.** (*Minnesota Historical Society*)

ABOVE:
Michilimackinac
State Park attracted
a growing number of
campers in the early
twentieth century.
OPPOSITE: The
majestic Mackinac
Bridge crosses the
Straits near recon-
structed Fort
Michilimackinac.

inac as a park, thus protecting it from devel-
opment. Conkling's foresight has paid great
dividends. His lots sold slowly and the
town did not begin to develop until the
railroad reached Mackinaw City in 1881.
Despite its location, the town remained
small and today has fewer than 1,000 residents. But the village does have wide, pleasing streets
and the site of the fort is still a park.

Originally named "Wawatam Park" in honor of
the Ojibwa Chief who had protected Alexander
Henry during the 1763 uprising, the fort site was a
favorite place for local folks to picnic and dig for
beads or other buried eighteenth-century artifacts.
These potholes destroyed a considerable amount of
valuable archaeological evidence and left large gaps
in our knowledge of Michilimackinac's past. The
town, however, retained its historical consciousness:
many of the streets are named for people who were
prominent in eighteenth-century Michilimackinac
history (although the spellings were not always
accurate).

Michigan's first state park had been created on
Mackinac Island in 1895 and the Mackinac Island
State Park Commission had been appointed to
administer it. In 1904, Mackinaw City turned their
park over to the State of Michigan. In 1909, the
State Legislature transferred the land to the Park
Commission and created the Michilimackinac State
Park. The Park Commission had no money to devel-
op the park, but they did have it surveyed, thus docu-
menting some of the surviving fort features.

During the 1920s improved roads and automobiles
brought people to Mackinaw City in great numbers.
To accommodate the influx of tourists, the Park

Commission developed Michilimackinac State Park into a picnic and camping park. After Chris Schneider, then Park Manager, located the remains of the stockade walls, the Commission decided to reconstruct the fort as a tourist attraction. When historic maps were compared with the newly found stockade, it was discovered that the west side of the fort site was still privately owned. The private lands were purchased and several streets were vacated by the village so that the fort could be reconstructed on its original site. The available stockade poles were shorter than the originals, but the Commission proceeded, and the reconstructed fort was dedicated on July 1, 1933. A few concession buildings and monuments, as well as a Civil War cannon, were placed in the fort and visitors wandered around at will.

Beginning in 1959, the fort was transformed. A few years earlier, the Mackinac Island State Park Commission had been given legislative authority to sell revenue bonds to finance historical developments. The

initial bond proceeds were spent installing a museum in Fort Mackinac. A modest admission charge generated sufficient monies to pay back the borrowed funds. With such success the Commission began to consider the possibility of a new reconstruction at Michilimackinac. With great foresight, they decided that professional archaeology should be done prior to reconstruction. Michigan State University was contracted to begin excavations in the summer of 1959. Based on existing maps, they selected the parade ground as the location of the initial dig. As they dug, expecting to find an unoccupied space, archaeologists came down upon the foundations of the 1769 soldiers' barracks. Obviously, additional historical research was needed. Historians soon located information about the barracks, including the original construction contract.

The archaeological and historical research proved so fruitful that it was decided to move ahead quickly to reconstruct the fort. The Commission expeditiously authorized an additional bond issue. Plans were developed to reconstruct the stockade and the soldiers' barracks with an interpretive museum inside. After a frantic construction season and with only the east half of the palisade reconstructed, the fort opened on June 26, 1960. Over 150,000 paid admissions were collected that summer.

One of the reasons for the strong attendance was the new four-lane highway (I-75), which had been constructed to Mackinaw City, and the spectacular Mackinac Bridge, which opened on November 1, 1957 to span the Straits. The one-way fare of $3.75 made some people reluctant to cross the bridge. Instead they stayed in Mackinaw City and many of them toured the newly reconstructed fort. Encouraged by the positive public reaction, the Commission reconstructed additional buildings as archaeologists uncovered their foundations.

The site is one of the longest ongoing excavations in the United States, with archaeologists excavating every summer since 1959. After working with MSU archaeologists for a number of years, the Mackinac Island State Park hired a staff archaeologist in 1970. Historical research also continued, resulting in many publications. Thousands of books and hundreds of reels of microfilm were added to the research library, providing a solid foundation for continued analysis. An archaeological laboratory was set up and over a million excavated artifacts

OPPOSITE: The reconstruction of Fort Michilimackinac began in the spring of 1960. BELOW: All the dirt excavated at Michilimackinac is carefully screened to find the smallest artifact.

ABOVE: Archaeological excavations are conducted every summer as they have been since 1959. OPPOSITE ABOVE: The sloop *Welcome* under reconstruction OPPOSITE RIGHT: Billowing sails propel the *Welcome*. OPPOSITE BELOW: Old Mackinac Point Lighthouse

have been cleaned, catalogued, stored, and entered into a computerized database. All of these resources are available to serious researchers as well as Park staff.

Adjacent to the State Park was the 1892 Old Mackinac Point Lighthouse. After the Mackinac Bridge was constructed the lighthouse was no longer needed by the U. S. Coast Guard, because navigational lights had been placed on the bridge. In 1960 the lighthouse was turned over to the Mackinac Island State Park Commission for use as a maritime museum. Exhibits were arranged in the ground floor and the museum was opened in 1972. A major focal point of the Maritime Park was the ongoing reconstruction of John Askin's 1775 sloop *Welcome*. The

keel of the replica was laid in 1972 and the hull was launched in 1980. Docked in the Mackinaw City Marina, she was rigged and sailed her maiden voyage in 1981. As is common with wooden boats, she began to rot and required extensive maintenance and repairs. In 1989 the *Welcome* was leased to the Maritime Heritage Alliance in Traverse City, where she is being repaired and fitted out to sail again.

By the late 1980s, the exhibits in the lighthouse needed refurbishing, so the museum was closed. Plans are currently underway for a restoration of the building and the installation of new exhibits when funding is available.

BELOW: Enthusiastic guides present lively interpretive programs to Colonial Michilimackinac visitors. OPPOSITE: The British red ensign waves over the reconstructed eighteenth-century village.

Visitors Today

WEATHER DETERMINES THE PATTERN of life at Colonial Michilimackinac in the same way as it did in the past. Summer is the busy season, when many people come to the area. Winter is much slower. Visitors come from all over the world: people from over sixty countries have signed the guest registers. Though the nearby states predominate, the park sees visitors from all fifty states, and people from Michigan comprise about half of the guests. Many of today's visitors have homes in the same region as the villages of the Native peoples who

traded furs in the eighteenth century. Because Michilimackinac is a gathering place, its history parallels the history of the entire upper Great Lakes region.

Colonial Michilimackinac is open from early May to mid-October and welcomes over 100,000 guests annually. Sometimes during January and February the fort opens on a Thursday, Friday, and Saturday to provide opportunities for school children and others to experience the rigors of a frontier winter. Interpretive staff take the Michilimackinac experience to schools throughout Michigan, following the routes of the fur traders of long ago. Each year presentations are made to more than 11,000 students in over 100 schools.

When you come to Colonial Michilimackinac today, you enter the Visitor Center underneath the Mackinac Bridge approach. The Visitor Center is located where Lakes Michigan and Huron come together. Immediately

inside the lobby is a thirty-five-foot-long birch bark *Canot de Maître* canoe, which was the primary mode of transportation in the eighteenth century. After you purchase your ticket, view the twelve-minute audio-visual program in the theatre, which presents an introductory overview of life at Michilimackinac. Nearby is one of our greatest treasures – the silver bowl ordered for Major Arent Schuyler DePeyster when he left Michilimackinac in 1779.

A spectacular view of Lake Michigan greets you as you follow the pathway to the fort. You pass through the "suburbs" area, where archaeologists have excavated several row houses and have located additional chimney and house sites with remote sensing equipment. A great deal remains to be learned about this area.

Before you reach the fort, you will encounter an encampment of Native people who have come to Michilimackinac to trade and to council. A fire is often burning either outside or inside the bark-covered *waginogan*. Enter the hut and you will realize how cozy it is, even in the winter. You can stay as long as you wish, learning about the Native way of life. This campsite represents the hundreds of similar encampments that dotted the beach during the height of the trading season.

Beyond you looms the eighteen-foot-high log stockade, which protects the people living inside. Sentry boxes surmount each bastion. Imagine soldiers in the boxes, who would have had an excellent view of your approach. The path along the lakeshore leads to the Water Gate, the entrance on the lake side of the fort. Before turning into the fort, note the small salute cannon, which is used for periodic firing demonstrations.

Passing into the fort through the Water Gate, you enter the world of the 1770s when Michilimackinac was at its peak size. Slightly over half of the ground inside the fort has been archaeologically excavated, and approximately one-third of the fort's buildings have been reconstructed. Use your imagination to fill the grassy areas with houses. Take the stairs up to the catwalk that encircles the fort. If you walk all the way around, it is more than a quarter of a mile, and you will get a good sense of the size and layout of the fort. Most of the reconstruction has been done in the northwest quadrant of the fort; this area gives you an idea of the crowded nature of the community. Immediately inside the Water Gate is the King's Store-

house, constructed by British soldiers in 1773 to store the soldiers' provisions and presents to be given to Native peoples. The original cobblestone floor is visible in the storage cellar.

The *Rue Dauphine* ("Street of the Princess") runs through the center of the fort from the Water Gate to the Land Gate. Across the street to the left is the Commanding Officer's House. Here Robert Rogers, Arent Schuyler DePeyster, Patrick Sinclair, and other British Commandants lived

OPPOSITE: The well-stocked, recon-structed King's Storehouse provides a glimpse of the orig-inal storage cellar floor. LEFT: A British soldier warms him-self in front of a fire-place in the recon-structed Soldiers' Barracks.

with their families. From his front porch the com-manding officer could keep a close watch on the Parade Ground and the Soldiers' Barracks. The Sol-diers' Barracks was the first building discovered by archaeologists and the first building reconstructed. A new exhibit about British soldiers at Michilimack-inac was installed in 1999.

Immediately behind the Soldiers' Barracks is the Guardhouse. Originally constructed by French sol-diers in 1751, it reflects a French architectural style. The Guardhouse was the headquarters for the sol-diers on guard duty. Here they ate, slept, and kept watch over any prisoners locked in the "black hole" dungeon beneath the floor.

To the north of the Guardhouse is a row of three French houses. Originally there were five houses in the row, but the two on the east end have not yet been excavated. They are being left as a preserve for future archaeologists. The Piquet House is used for British cooking and family life demonstration. The Askin House is set up to show the house of a wealthy

Colonial Michilimackinac **95**

British trader such as John Askin who may have lived here. The Chevalier House is used as the entrance to an exciting underground archaeological tunnel exhibit, "Treasures from the Sand." Many of the eighteenth-century artifacts found since 1959 are on display, as well as the preserved remains of a British house basement and the original French well. For those unable to walk down the steps, an audio-visual presentation about the exhibition is available in the Askin House.

The Military Latrine is in the northwest corner of the fort. Constructed by the British army, it had separate sections for officers and enlisted men. The French did not build outhouses but disposed of their night soil by throwing it into the back yards. This corner of the fort was called the "St. Joseph Bastion" because canoes coming and going to Fort St. Joseph in southern Michigan followed the shoreline to the west.

The Priest's House, originally constructed in the 1740s, features two connected storage cellars which can be viewed from the underground

"Treasures from the Sand" exhibit. The Priest's House is connected to the church by a covered passageway. Because the blacksmith worked for the priest, the Blacksmith Shop is in close proximity. Visitors can watch

the smith fashion ironwork for use in the reconstruction of Michilimackinac.

The Church of Ste. Anne de Michilimackinac, originally erected in 1743 by master carpenter Joseph Ainse and moved to Mackinac Island in 1780, was the center of religious activities in the community. As was the custom, some of the prominent citizens were buried beneath the church floor. Archaeologists found a portion of the original church bell on this site. Today the ringing of the bell signals the beginning of an eighteenth-century wedding re-enactment. The church is available for private weddings after the fort is closed.

The Southwest Row House originally contained six houses. Three have been reconstructed. Charles Langlade lived in the middle house, where today interpreters demonstrate French cooking and culture. A craftsmen's shop and a trading store are located in the other houses. Stairways provide access to the

ABOVE: Costumed interpreters help visitors connect with the past.

OPPOSITE TOP: Many of the artifacts discovered by archaeologists are on display in the underground exhibit "Treasures from the Sand."

OPPOSITE BOTTOM: The priest's house interior

Colonial Michilimackinac **97**

attic area. The porch faces the church and the benches are a good place to rest. Kitchen gardens located at the rear of the houses are enclosed with a typical French five-foot-high cedar palisade fence. These back fences run along the *Rue du Diable* ("Street of the Devil"), which fronts the South/Southwest Row House. The King's Garden, at the east end of this row, formerly the site of the French Commandant's house, was used to grow provisions for the soldiers.

An original French fireplace, once part of Michael Amelin's house, was preserved when blowing sand covered it and a pine tree grew over the top. Now uncovered by archaeologists, it is preserved under a small shed. Most of the South/Southwest Row House has been excavated and its walls are marked out on the ground. The eastern end of the Row House is being excavated by staff archaeologists. You are invited to watch the painstaking but fascinating process and see

the past uncovered before your eyes. All of the dirt is carefully screened to find even the smallest bead or seed. Each excavation unit is carefully mapped and photographed. The differences in soil color show where walls or other features were located. All this information is plotted on maps that slowly reveal the eighteenth-century fur trading community. Interpreters welcome your questions and will be pleased to show you the latest discoveries. When the archaeology is complete, the park's long-range plan calls for the reconstruction of the entire Row House, which will be used to present the history of the Michilimackinac community.

There is another cluster of reconstructed buildings in the southeast quadrant of the fort. Walking along the *Rue de Babillarde* ("Street of the Gossip") you come to the Chevalier House. This is the most eastern building of the South/Southeast Row House and is the only portion to be excavated. The Chevalier House, originally built in the 1730s, became quite dilapidated and was torn down in 1775. Today the building serves as the entrance to the underground Powder Magazine. A stairway leads down to an exhibition about firearms at Michilimackinac and connects to the adjacent Powder Magazine. The Powder Magazine was originally constructed in the 1740s to store gunpowder. It was built beneath ground level to lessen damage if it exploded. Originally privately owned, it was taken over by the British military. When the British moved to Mackinac Island, they burned the building to keep it from falling into enemy hands. The collapsed dirt roof smothered the fire and preserved the charred floorboards. You can see the original floorboards and wall posts, which have been carefully preserved.

Across the street, two houses of the six-unit Southeast Row House have been reconstructed. The British Officer's House, originally built as two houses,

OPPOSITE TOP: Corn was a staple food at Michilimackinac. OPPOSITE BOTTOM: Even the smallest bead or seed has a story to tell. BELOW: Most objects found by archaeologists are broken, but some can be pieced together.

was owned by French-Canadian fur traders and then rented to British soldiers. During the 1770s a British officer, Lieutenant George Clowes, lived here. Gold-plated King's 8th buttons were found during the excavation. The building is now set up to show how a British officer lived at the post.

Next door is the house purchased from old Pierre Parent in 1765 by merchants Ezekiel Solomon and Gershon Levy. They used the east room for living quarters and operated their trading store out of the west room. The preserved remnants of the storage cellar and the logs of the wall are visible in the west room.

The front of the houses opens onto the Parade Ground used by the soldiers for drill. Today it is the location of musket firing demonstrations. Flying from the tall wooden flagpole is the British Red Ensign with the Union Jack in the corner. This was the usual British flag used in the upper Great Lakes area. The Parade Ground and the northeast quadrant of the fort are now open space. However, in the 1770s the area was ringed by houses on both the east and north side. There was a large vacant yard to the east of the Commanding Officer's House where a French house had been demolished. This area has not yet been excavated.

Exiting the fort by the Land Gate, you can imagine the Ojibwa rushing through this gate in 1763 when they captured the fort. Immediately outside the fort is the open area where the famous *baggatiway* game took place. The small houses in this area are not on original sites but have been erected to represent the "suburbs" outside the fort. Built in a French architectural style, they are not open to the public.

Behind the houses is a corral for horses and cows and a sheep pen. These are located near where Augustin Langlade had his stables in the 1740s. Close by, a small orchard grows. Apple trees were planted at Michilimackinac in the eighteenth century and some were transplanted to Mackinac Island when the community moved.

Michilimackinac is a place to be experienced and enjoyed. You can zip through in an hour or spend half a day. Periodically during the summer, appropriate re-enactment groups are permitted to camp in the "suburbs" area between the palisade and the parking lot. Dressed in eighteenth-cen-

tury attire, staying in tents, and cooking over open fires, they remind visitors of the large numbers of people who gathered at Michilimackinac during its heyday. Like the traders of old, they come from far away for a summer rendezvous at the historic gathering place of the upper Great Lakes.

Before you leave, check out the museum store, where many eighteenth-century replicas will provide reminders of your visit. An extensive array of books for all ages contains additional information about life on the colonial frontier. A number of these books were written by park staff and other researchers using the archaeological and historical information that has made possible the reconstruction of Michilimackinac.

OPPOSITE: Gold-plated King's 8th officer's button from the 1770s

ABOVE: Guests join interpreters in a lively wedding celebration dance.

Colonial Michilimackinac **101**

Colonial Michilimackinac connects the past and the present. Stand on the catwalk and let your imagination catch a whisper of conversations from the past.

The Future

COLONIAL MICHILIMACKINAC IS a living historical park. Much has been accomplished but much remains to be done. Nearly half of the interior of the fort has yet to be excavated and only a very small portion of the "suburbs" has been archaeologically tested. The nearby Odawa village has not yet been located and some related but remote sites warrant further investigation. Historians have gathered copies of thousands of manuscript records but many more are known to exist in repositories around the world. Manuscripts relating to the French occupation promise to provide the most new insights. Conducting historical research is like putting together a jigsaw puzzle whose pieces have been scattered all over the world. They have to be located, copied, and analyzed.

New insights gained from ongoing research will undergird the refurbishing of older exhibits and provide new information for our costumed interpreters. Our goal is not simply to learn about the past but to share it with others in a wide variety of ways. The next building to be reconstructed is the South/Southwest Row House. It will house an interpretive exhibition detailing the coming together of peoples at Michilimackinac. When you next return to Colonial Michilimackinac, look for the changes and improvements as the past comes to life.

For Further Reading

Publications of Mackinac State Historic Parks,
Mackinac Island, Michigan

GENFRAL

Armour, David A., *Fort Michilimackinac Sketchbook*. 1975.

------ Editor, *Treason? At Michilimackinac: The Proceedings of a General Court Martial held in Montreal in October, 1768, for the Trial of Major Robert Rogers*. 1967.

------Editor, *Attack at Michilimackinac: Alexander Henry's Travels and Adventures in Canada and the Indian Territories between the Years 1760 and 1764*. 1971.

Armour, David A., and Keith R. Widder, *At the Crossroads: Michilimackinac During the American Revolution*. 1978.

Dunnigan, Brian Leigh, *The Necessity of Regularity in Quartering Soldiers*. 1999.

Eustice, Sally, *History From the Hearth: A Colonial Michilimackinac Cookbook*. 1997.

Gringhuis, Dirk, *The Lore of the Great Turtle: Indian Legends of Mackinac Retold*. 1970.

------Were-Wolves and Will-O-the-Wisps: French Tales of Mackinac Retold*. 1974.

------The Young Voyageur*. 1969.

May, George S., Editor, *The Doctor's Secret Journal*. 1960.

Petersen, Eugene T., *Michilimackinac and the Porcelain City*. 1985.

Porter, Phil, *Mackinac: An Island Famous in These Regions*. 1998.

Stone, Lyle M., *Fort Michilimackinac, 1715-1781: An Archaeological Perspective on the Revolutionary Frontier*. 1974.

MACKINAC HISTORY, VOLUME II

Armour, David A., *David and Elizabeth: The Mitchell Family of the Straits of Mackinac*. 1982.

Dunnigan, Brian Leigh, *Milestones of the Past: Military Buttons and Insignia from Mackinac*. 1975.

Gerin-Lajoie, Marie, Translator, *Fort Michilimackinac in 1749: Lotbinière's Plan and Description*. 1976.

Gringhuis, Dirk, *Indian Costume at Mackinac: Seventeenth and Eighteenth Century*. 1972.

REPORTS IN MACKINAC HISTORY AND ARCHAEOLOGY

Dunnigan, Brian Leigh, *King's Men at Mackinac: The British Garrisons, 1780-1796*. 1973.

Hamilton, T. M., *Firearms on the Frontier: Guns at Fort Michilimackinac, 1715-1781*. 1976.

Heldman, Donald P. and William L. Minnerly, *The Powder Magazine at Fort Michilimackinac: Excavation Report*. 1977.

ARCHAEOLOGICAL COMPLETION REPORT SERIES

Adams, Diane L., *Lead Seals from Fort Michilimackinac, 1715-1781*. 1989.

Frurip, David J., Russell Malewicki and Donald P. Heldman, *Colonial Nails from Michilimackinac: Differentiation by Chemical and Statistical Analysis*. 1983.

Halchin, Jill Y., *Excavations at Fort Michilimackinac, 1983-1985: House C of the Southeast Row House, The Solomon-Levy-Parant House*. 1985.

Hamilton, T. M., and K. O. Emery, *Eighteenth-Century Gunflints from Fort Michilimackinac and other Colonial Sites*. 1988.

Hauser, Judith Ann, *Jesuit Rings from Fort Michilimackinac and Other European Contact Sites*. 1982.

Heldman, Donald P., *Archaeological Investigations at French Farm Lake in Northern Michigan, 1981-1982: A British Colonial Farm Site*. 1983.

Morand, Lynn L., *Craft Industries at Fort Michilimackinac, 1715-1781*. 1994.

Scott, Elizabeth M., *French Subsistence at Fort Michilimackinac, 1715-1781: The Clergy and the Traders*. 1985.

Whitaker, John M. F., *The Functions of Four Colonial Yards of the Southeast Row House, Fort Michilimackinac, Michigan*. 1998.

Williams, J. Mark, and Gary Shapiro, *A Search for the Eighteenth Century Village at Michilimackinac: A Soil Resistivity Survey*. 1982.

With Michigan State University Press

Peyser, Joseph L., translator and editor, *Jacques Legardeur de Saint-Pierre: Officer, Gentleman, Entrepreneur*. 1996.

------ Translator and editor, *On the Eve of the Conquest: The Chevalier de Raymond's Critique of New France in 1754*. 1997.